A PALETTE FOR THE PEOPLE

The Kresge Eminent Artist Award honors an exceptional artist in the visual, performing or literary arts for lifelong professional achievements and dedication to metropolitan Detroit's cultural community.

Shirley Woodson is the 2021 Kresge Eminent Artist.

This monograph celebrates her life and work.

COVER (DETAIL) AND FOLLOWING PAGE
Bather with Angel Wing
2006
Acrylic on Canvas
36 x 40 in.

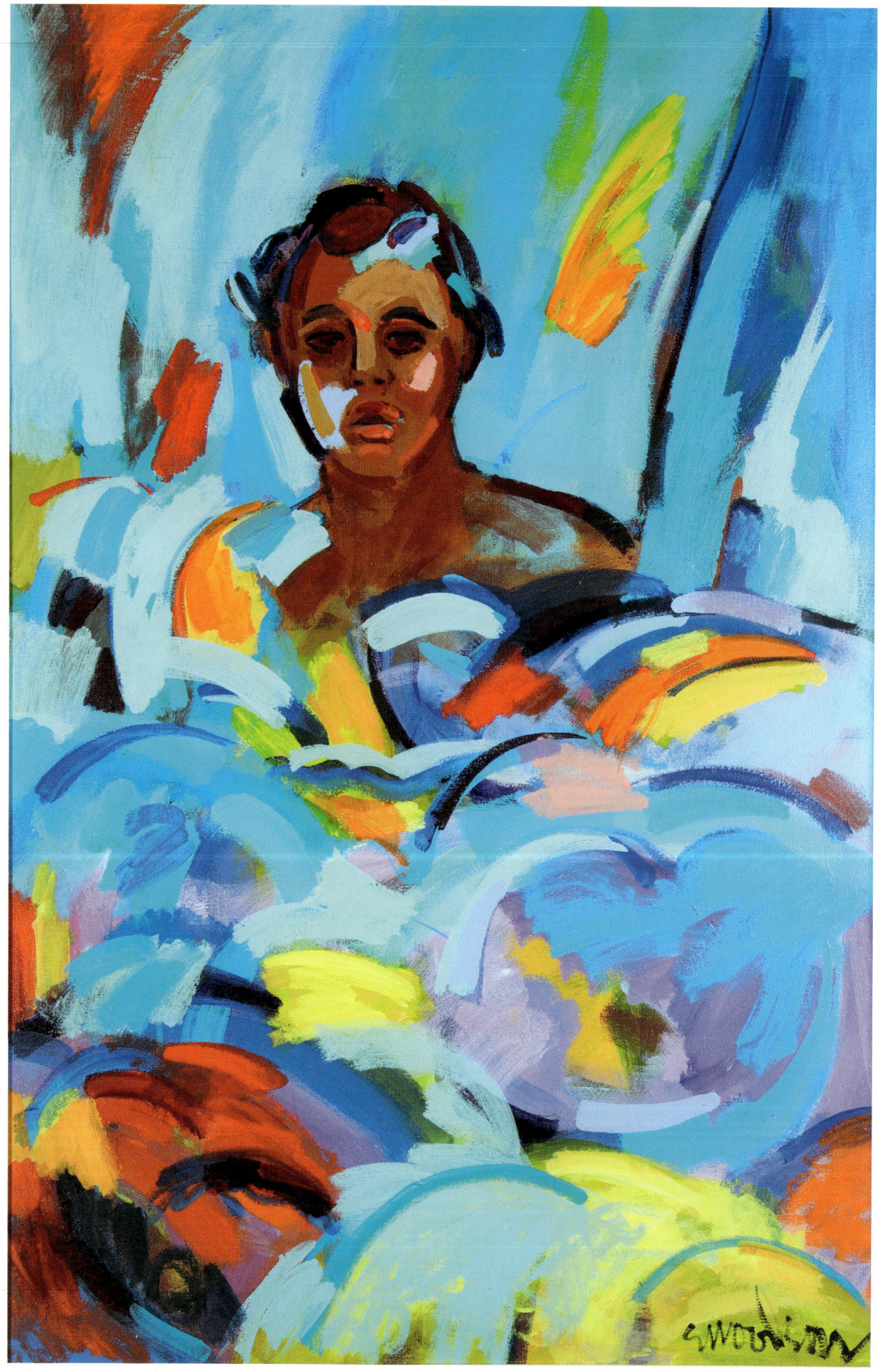

A PALETTE FOR THE PEOPLE

The Vibrant World of Shirley Woodson

Nichole Christian, editor
Patrick Barber, art director

with contributions from Camille Brewer, Allie McGhee, Dell Pryor, Jocelyn Rainey, Senghor Reid and Yvette Rock.

Contents

Foreword
Rip Rapson   **6**

Artist Statement
Shirley Woodson   **9**

Rooted in Bold
How figurative painter Shirley Woodson stretched beyond her own canvas to create a more vibrant world for generations of Black artists.
Nichole Christian   **10**

Select Works, Projects and Awards **70**

Our Congratulations **74**

The Kresge Eminent Artist Award and Winners **76**

Index **78**

List of Works **80**

In the Tradition
Six artists, former students and community leaders explore selected pieces of Shirley Woodson's work.

Her Eye Watches
Renowned painter and long-time friend **Allie McGhee** on the message beyond Shirley Woodson's vision of brilliant color. **33**

Carrying it On
Contemporary textile art curator and art historian **Camille Brewer** on the long reach of Shirley Woodson's multifaceted practice. **36**

The Giver
Legendary gallerist and Detroit arts doyenne **Dell Pryor** on the disciplined endurance of Shirley Woodson. **40**

Orbiting Shirley
Children's art gallery owner and multi-media artist **Yvette Rock** on her mentor's layered approach to making a life of meaning. **44**

Inheritance
Painter, arts teacher and gallerist **Jocelyn Rainey** on Shirley Woodson as a culture-shaping warrior for other Black women visual artists. **48**

A Son Sees Best
2009 Kresge Artist Fellow, painter and art instructor **Senghor Reid** offers an intimate view of his mother's legacy and her impact on his work. **52**

Salon
Curated selections from various themed series painted by Shirley Woodson beginning in the 1960s.

Flights, Crossroads and Journeys **56**

Bathers and the Sea **58**

Ancestors Known and Unknown **60**

The Painter and The Poet
A look at Shirley Woodson's collaboration with legendary poet and Broadside Press publisher Dudley Randall.
Nichole Christian **64**

Shirley Collects
An exploration of the painter and educator's other great love, art collecting.
Nichole Christian **68**

Foreword

For those of us open to its possibilities, art has been an indispensible source of solace in our impossibly difficult recent times. Among the works I've turned to have been the works of our past Kresge Eminent Artists—to the poems and photographs, music and textiles, paintings and ceramics.

Each of our Eminent Artists has offered something to help us carry on with our lives even as the fabric of our sociality has been frayed. They've helped me stay grounded in the common purpose of community. They've helped keep me rooted in tradition and hopeful for the future.

In Shirley Woodson, our 2021 Kresge Eminent Artist, our 13th since 2008, we have, again, an artist who exemplifies a lifetime of excellence and achievement in her art forms and contributions to the artistic and cultural communities of metropolitan Detroit. In Shirley Woodson, we have another artist who offers sustenance for these hard times—an artist who offers us beauty and hard truths, inquiry and hope.

Shirley is an artist who offers us a singular vision that is also universally embracing. She leads us both gently and forcefully into the world of her vibrant color palette with imagery that flows particularly and unapologetically from the African American experience to speak to the world. Whether the work is abstract, figurative, or something of a blend, her creations are always captivating—moments frozen in elusive, larger narratives that leave us wanting more.

Beyond the canvas she has been an exemplary arts teacher and arts administrator in Detroit and Highland Park, and, as such, an advocate for robust arts education and for the long overdue inclusion of African American artists to enrich syllabi and the canon. She has not only inspired artists but mentored them as well. And as we have seen so often in artists such as Shirley, selflessly paying it forward can yield returns for wider and wider circles of beneficiaries.

These times of turmoil make evermore clear the ways in which artists like Shirley, through art and activism, fortify our entire community.

—**RIP RAPSON**
PRESIDENT AND CEO
THE KRESGE FOUNDATION

Shield of the Nile No. 2
1984
Acrylic on canvas
71 x 103½ in.

Aretha the Queen

1970

Oil on linen

36 x 36 in.

Artist Statement

Paintings are my diaries.

Drawings are my prose.

Collage is my poetry.

Assemblages are my dialogues.

All the threads of my life have been about art and its ability to connect and create ways of showing the beauty, the history and the necessity of all art but particularly Black art.

This journey has been my life, and it continues to move me.

I'm still creating and discovering.

—2021 KRESGE EMINENT ARTIST SHIRLEY WOODSON

ROOTED IN BOLD

How figurative painter Shirley Woodson stretched beyond her own canvas to create a more vibrant world for generations of Black artists

Nichole Christian

Self Portrait with Teeth

1963

Oil on Linen

18 × 38 in.

Shirley Woodson cannot be compressed. She will not be constrained. She is not one thing. She is multiple creative movements at once, by choice. For life.

Attempt to know Woodson through a single label—even the one for which she is nationally known, that of a prolific figurative painter—and much of what makes her an enduring artistic force gets lost. The real art of Woodson comes into view only by stepping back and staring at the interlocking frames of a life centered on building access for others while endeavoring to build a career of her own.

Make no mistake: Woodson the painter wants you to see her works, to engage with them closely and to keep up with the evolution of her practice and ideas if you can. She has literally painted hundreds upon hundreds of oils and acrylics, typically working on several at once, her preferred method of making. She's poured nearly as much time and passion into creating photo-based collages, assemblages and drawings. The two-room studio that Woodson has maintained in Northwest Detroit since 2003, with her son Senghor, also a celebrated painter, teems with the evidence of a life completely given to artistic expression and a fierce unending discipline.

Nearly every inch of space, floor to ceiling, is occupied with stacks of in-progress canvases and framed paintings for the various eras of her work, dating back to the 1960s. Woodson, a member since childhood of Detroit's St Stephen AME, could easily be the physical embodiment of the classic spiritual lyric *I don't feel no ways tired*. At 85, art still intrigues and moves her. "Art is vital," she says. "It's something I understood early on as a child, and it's never changed." She continues to create, beginning new canvases, adding to others in progress, doing so daily some weeks, and during a pandemic no less.

The marvel of Woodson could end here with a just celebration of longevity for a woman who chose her path early, at age 7, and has spent more than seven decades rigorously honoring its twists and triumphs.

But Shirley Woodson's story is bolder by design. Her actions beyond her studio are arguably boldest of all. "We certainly need to applaud who she is as an incredible fine

Shirley in 1975.

artist," says John Bolden, a retired executive vice chancellor at Wayne County Community College District who's known Woodson for nearly 30 years. "Her talent is unquestionable. But what's most remarkable is how committed and consistent she has been about bringing culture to the community and making sure that it is reflective and of the highest quality."

Look across the roles of Woodson's creative life—that of fine arts painter, art educator and mentor, historian and collector—one sees the same mark. Woodson has lived a life dedicated to uplifting the beauty of Black art and breaking barriers of exclusion along the way.

At first glance, one might deem the mission mightier than the woman. Woodson is petite with a sharp preference for quiet elegant ways. Yet she speaks about art, not only Black art, with the vigor and precision of a towering, focused master.

"My study of art history gave me a fantastic range of the way artists work, and other ways art has kept silent about our contributions."

Turning her knowledge of art into a tool of community empowerment is the defining choice of Woodson's life. "I just thought 'What good was it for me to learn these things and not share them in a way that could benefit everyone?' Art is supposed to change the way we understand the world around us, even the difficult things about it." Generations of fellow artists, educators, rising Black art gallerists, collectors of her work and former students call themselves the beneficiaries of her bone-deep dedication.

Never has the chorus in honor of Woodson been louder than with her selection as the 2021 Kresge Eminent Artist. Shirley Woodson, supporters say, is worthy. "If she didn't make a piece of art at all and had only worked as an arts administrator who's done everything for so long to make sure other people could make art, and kids could have some real-life idea that there are such people, artists, out there, that would be enough to celebrate Shirley Woodson," explains Elizabeth Youngblood, a Detroit-based multidisciplinary artist and one of Woodson's former students at Tappan Junior High School.

Youngblood adds: "When you put together all that she's done for decades it's really profound to think that we're talking about one person in one lifetime."

Over the years, Bolden turned to Woodson for advice on ways to attract artists to the college's gallery and visiting artist workshops. "Every connection that she has and the immense knowledge she carries, she's always used for the benefit of the community. She's kept art moving."

To become *eminent*, say the five artists and arts professionals who selected Woodson as the 2021 Kresge Eminent Artist, is a marker of far more than talent. "Shirley Woodson's life journey has been one of extraordinary contribution to our local and national community—yes, as a brilliant visual artist, but also through her lifelong work as an arts educator, arts administrator and institution builder," says Dr. Gloria House, the 2019 Kresge Eminent Artist, and one of her selection panelists.

"How amazing that while she was so engaged in all of these tasks that strengthened our community, she was evolving her own gifts as an artist, progressively experimenting with various themes and styles, producing prolifically, and achieving an excellence that has won the esteem of her peers and collectors nationwide. We, the panelists, were very happy to affirm Shirley as the 2021 Kresge Eminent Artist," adds House.

Rip Rapson, the president and CEO of The Kresge Foundation, salutes Woodson, the 13th recipient, as an embodiment of the spirit of the award and the layered ways artists and the arts enhance life in metro Detroit. "Shirley Woodson has taught and mentored, cultivating and expanding creative opportunities for successive generations. She is an artist who leads by engaged example," Rapson says. "Her superlative technique is rooted in inviting the viewer to see the world in a different way, whether the work is abstract, figurative, or something of a blend. Her impact through all these channels underscores with enormous power the role that arts can, and do, play in building and preserving vibrant communities."

Self Portrait with Studio
1964
Oil on Linen
40 × 60 in.

15

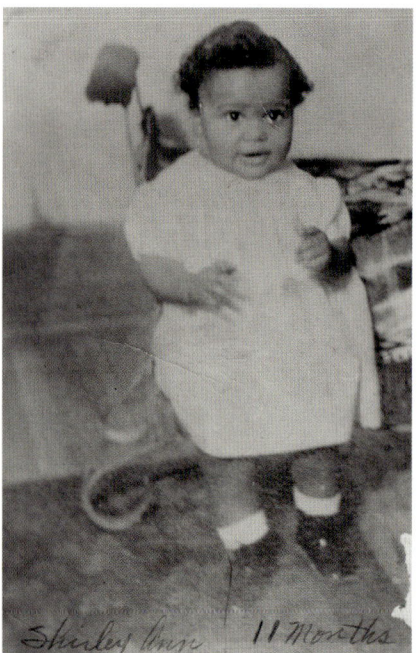

Shirley, 11 months, 1937.

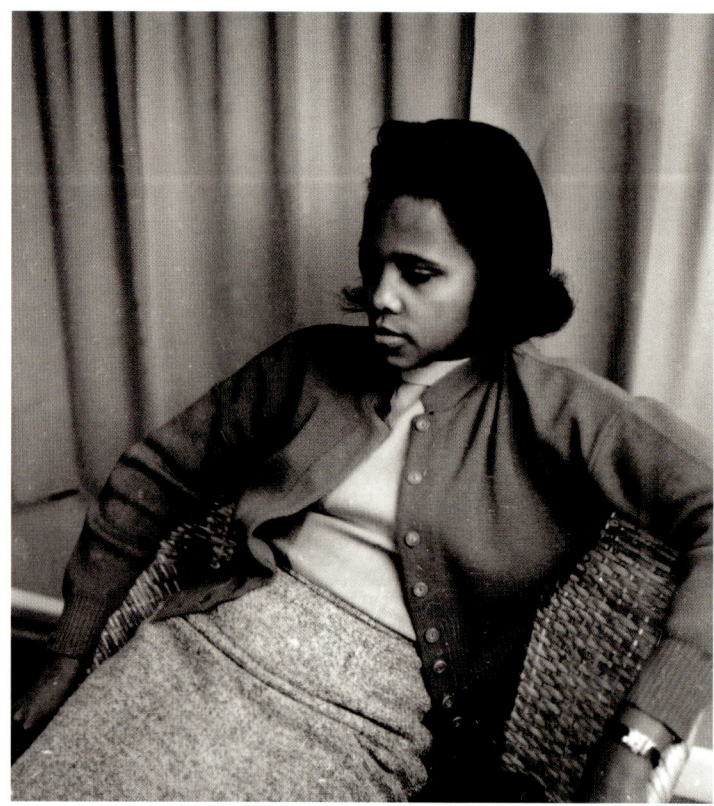

Shirley, early 1960s.

2

Call it an ironic detail of her life, one that could easily be cast aside except for the dimension it adds: Shirley Ann Woodson, the unapologetic maker of fine Black art and champion of Black arts opportunities, was born in the same city that cradled one of America's earliest and most violent white supremacist groups: Pulaski, Tennessee.

The Ku Klux Klan came first, on Christmas of 1865, when six Confederate Army veterans organized rules for the founding branch of the secret white society. A year later the men elected their first grand wizard, Confederate Gen. Nathan Bedford Forrest, who before the war made himself into one of the South's wealthiest men by way of slave-trading and owning cotton plantations.

By the time of Woodson's birth 70 years later, on March 3, 1936, Pulaski's reputation was irrevocably stained by violent acts of racial hatred and legalized separatism. A group of white vigilantes sparked a race riot in 1868. Six Black men died.

Pulaski never got the chance to directly scar or shortchange young Woodson. Her parents, Celia Trotter Woodson and Claude Woodson, made certain of that. Claude was four years older than the "unusual country girl" who would become his wife after they met at a Tennessee county fair. He was born and raised in Pulaski, while Celia, the youngest of 10 children, grew up 19 miles away on a family farm in a farming community called Liberty.

"They told me things about other people," she recalls. "But my parents never came face-to-face with any of the hatred. It was just one of those things—a reality you live with but it's not going to keep you from being alive or enjoying life. You just keep going—that's the story really of all of us, even now."

Wanting more for Shirley, and for themselves, the Woodsons moved north to Detroit's west side just three months after her birth. Three of Celia's older sisters—Emily, Azzie Lee and Charlotte—had already relocated to Detroit.

"All of those women came here and got jobs as housekeepers. As Black people often do, they also found other things to manage and create a life," Woodson says during a visit to her studio, where she pores over old photos and her family's early years in Detroit.

16 **Rooted in Bold**

Though the young family initially moved in with Woodson's Aunt Lee, it didn't take long before the economic promise of Detroit proved true for them, too. Claude had learned to be resourceful at an early age. When the Pulaski school he attended failed to offer Black students an option to graduate, he moved himself to Chattanooga where the education options were brighter and relatives had enough space to welcome him. After high school Claude returned to Pulaski with "excellent" math skills and became a bookkeeper at a funeral home owned by Celia's family.

Yet following the move to Detroit, Claude had to set those skills aside for a string of jobs — at one point he worked three which kept him away from the family for up to 12 hours a day. One of the jobs included picking up and delivering shirts, which Celia would wash and iron for white families. "My mother was very industrious. She used every skill she had," Woodson says. "There were no laundries back then, and white families needed ironing. So, she put a little ad in the newspaper."

A family business was born. "Black people always had other things that they were doing to manage. It was just part of the survival, the living, as they'd say." For Celia, that also meant keeping a close rein over the home.

By 1941, the Woodson family had welcomed a second child, Curtis, and had purchased their first home. "In those days, everyone wanted the same thing, I think, opportunity, opportunity. We found it in Detroit and never looked back. It's always been home."

Shirley with her brother, Curtis, and her parents, 1944.

Shirley sharing her work with parents, Claude and Celia Woodson. Arts Extended Gallery, on east Warren near John R in Detroit, early 1960s.

17

Shirley in cap and gown for her college graduation from Wayne State University, 1958.

Shirley painting with aerosols while working on her *Journeys* series, 1975.

OPPOSITE
Newspaper clipping dated March 17, 1962. Detroit artists Shirley Woodson, Alice Agee and Cledie Taylor visiting the Albright-Knox gallery in Buffalo, NY.

18

3 If Celia Woodson had painted a portrait of her little girl's journey into art — a life dedicated to making it and ultimately expanding its cultural accessibility — she would have undoubtedly begun with a pencil (not a brush) and a bare wall.

This is what Shirley Woodson always heard whenever she asked her late mother to help trace the origins of her creativity. "My mother said I was about 3 when I wrote all over the wall." The story goes that even at that young age, Woodson's strokes and scrawls were distinctive. Brazen.

"I guess that was my first mural," jokes Shirley. "Since we were in someone else's home, she said we got an eraser and she made me erase all of it. I'm not really sure that she had any problem with the art."

Woodson's earliest memory starts in kindergarten at the now-shuttered Detroit Columbian Elementary School. "I remember the art room so vividly; it was a downstairs room. I loved being there, just everything about it. It was a magical place."

Woodson's teachers witnessed the initial spark too. They set out to nurture it by selecting her for special art extension classes which, at the time, were available through a collaboration between Detroit Public Schools and the Detroit Institute of Arts (DIA). "I was in the art institute every Saturday from grade 7 through high school," Woodson says. "It was sort of my most favorite place to be. Whenever I left home, I wanted to go to the museum."

From that early exposure, Woodson discovered two pivotal lessons: the importance of learning to see and of establishing networks. In fact, it was there where she met a woman who would become a central and inspiring figure in her life, Dr. Cledie Taylor, a longtime Black arts historian, noted art educator and gallerist.

"I've known Shirley Woodson since she was a teenager," says Taylor, now in her early 90s and considered one of the three grande dames of Black art in Detroit, along with Woodson and iconic gallerist Dell Pryor. "I first encountered her there at the DIA. You could sense then that she had the makings of a very committed artist and that extra something, a fire."

Woodson traces much of her early love

Rooted in Bold

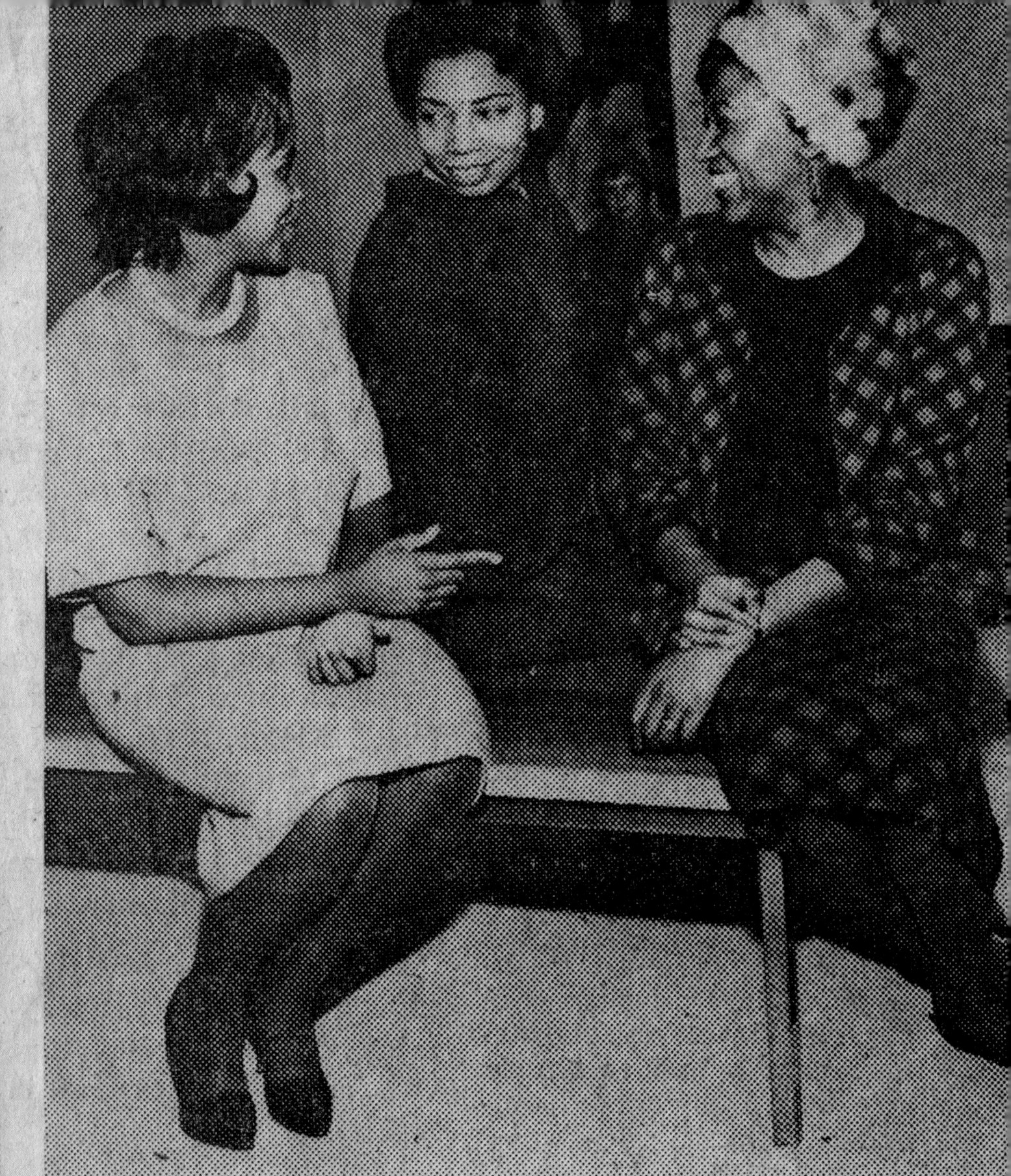

Discussing the Van Gogh exhibition they had just seen are Shirley Woodson, Mrs. Oliver (Alice) Agee, and Mrs. Lorenzo (Cledie) Taylor, all artists themselves.

March 17, 1967

Shirley surrounded by works in her collection: paintings to her right by Bob Thompson, etchings to her left by Henry Ossawa Tanner. Portrait of Shirley with Frank Bezenah by Robert Wilbert.

Shirley with sons Khari and Senghor at the African World Festival, Hart Plaza, Detroit, 1983.

for art to a twin love of learning. "I loved school. I was captivated by the classroom even through high school. I remember one day in high school, my little group arrived, and they told us there was no school that day because there'd been a water break." The group turned for home and along the way stopped to buy potato chips. Her companions relished the free time, but not Woodson: "I was mortified. I wanted to be in school."

Her reason ran deep: "I loved that you could go there and discover something new every day. That stuck with me."

While most of her friends at Detroit's Chadsey High School chose Latin and French as electives, teenage Woodson raced toward art, devouring every opportunity she could find including taking classes at other schools in the district, and becoming an award-winning student in the Detroit Public Schools Gifted and Talented Arts Program. "Art completely had me," she says. "I didn't know where it would take me, but I knew it was the only thing I wanted to do."

Unwavering support at home made the pursuit of an artist's life especially exciting: "Neither of my parents were artists, but they did have honest enjoyment and appreciation of culture. I didn't have to deal with doubt. It was never, 'Why do you want to be an artist?' They were more curious about the choices I was making in my paintings than who I wanted to become."

Woodson's passion for the classroom continued after high school, attending Wayne State University, where she earned a Bachelor of Fine Arts in 1958 and, nine years later, in 1965 a Master of Fine Arts degree. In between she completed graduate studies in painting and art history at the School of the Art Institute of Chicago, and independent art studies in Paris, Rome and Stockholm.

Both of Woodson's degrees were anchored by her early passion to paint, but college also revealed the need to steer that love into a career path. "I wanted people to see my art, but I also wanted to make money," she says. "I liked getting paid."

So, back to the classroom Woodson went. This time, she was the teacher. In a twist of fate, one of her first assignments as an art teacher in training was at Columbian Elementary School in the very basement classroom where art had first taken hold of her. "I knew then that I still loved school and that I had something I could now offer."

As a new teacher, Woodson wound her way through a number of Detroit schools including Tappan Junior High. "I remember her looking too close to our age, too young to be the teacher," recalls Youngblood, her former student at Tappan during the 1960s. "I also remember how much fun she brought. Shirley believed in me making art before I did."

Woodson the educator distinguished herself first and perhaps longest while working for Highland Park Schools. She spent nearly 27 years teaching art and guiding the arts curriculum for the district and the now-defunct Highland Park Community College.

"You didn't have to be an art teacher to be amazed by the difference Shirley Woodson brought to the classroom," says Paralee Day, a former reading specialist for Highland Park Schools who has known Woodson nearly 50 years.

"Clearly she was a superior artist with techniques she taught to students. But what was fun to watch was the joy in her classroom. I'm so happy to see Kresge celebrate the whole of who she is including teaching. The other Eminent Artists are in good company having Shirley join them."

Robin McDaniel is a retired Detroit Public Schools art teacher. In her retirement, she's become a focused artist, something she credits to her days working under Woodson in her final public education role as the district's supervisor of fine arts from 1992 to 2008.

"Her soul is so good. She fought as hard for her teachers to have the best resources as she did for the students," recalls McDaniel, a printmaker and past president of the district's art teachers' association. It was Woodson who insisted that art teachers learn to develop workshops showcasing their specific media and that they have seats on the district's book selection committee.

"She knew that the art books we were using didn't represent the Brown and Black students that we were teaching. There were no references to Jacob Lawrence or Elizabeth Catlett. This was Shirley's way of doing something about it and something that ultimately helped us do our jobs a lot better in terms of giving students a true picture."

Postcard advertising a show at the JRainey Gallery, 2000. Front row, from left: Shirley Woodson, Gilda Snowden, Camille Brewer. Back row, from left: Valerie Fair, Anita Bates, Sabrina Nelson.

Shirley in her home studio at her parents' house, 1988.

A splash of Shirley's favorite color, from one of her paintings.

Step back far enough and one sees parallels between Shirley Woodson's style as an arts education administrator and how she approaches her life as a painter. "From a distance, she's this gentle soldier kindly nudging ideas and people along," McDaniel says. "Really, Shirley is a fighter who's very disciplined about what she does and believes. She sees the possibilities before you do, and she has a way of helping you see too."

McDaniel always marveled at how seamlessly Woodson maintained her individual art practice with a busy day job expanding opportunities for students and teachers. Under her leadership, a number of popular and competitive student exhibition programs developed and grew, including annual showcases at the Fisher Building—one of Detroit's iconic Albert Kahn skyscrapers—and the DIA. McDaniel often thinks back to her days with Woodson as a supervisor and encourager. "We were her students really," she says. "She showed us firsthand how to be a great art teacher *and* an artist. As women, especially Black women, we sometimes let the things we love take a back seat."

But not Woodson. "Shirley is that bold example that you *can* have a life as an artist while you're all of these other things," McDaniel says.

"She's still flying."

4

Red is Shirley Woodson's favorite color.

She infuses a splash or hint of it in every work she creates. Sometimes it exists as an undertone detectable only to the eyes of other trained artists. For Woodson, red is a source of energy, a coded primary reminder that everything, even beauty, needs a solid foundation.

With two art degrees, Woodson thought she had the foundation for a life as a real living, thriving artist.

Her awakening was stark and transformative. The art world was being forced to broaden its eyes too by the dawning of the Black Arts Movement, from the late 1950s through the early 1970s. Detroit's soaring Black population made the city a natural hotbed of unapologetic pride and creative expression.

In fact, the African American poet and author Langston Hughes, traveled to Detroit in February 1964 to help celebrate a series of Negro History Week events. During his visit, he helped fundraise for an African American gallery at the Detroit Institute of Arts, according to art historian Julia R. Myers and her book, *Harold Neal and Detroit African American Artists, 1945 Through the Black Arts Movement.* (Woodson is one of 10 Black artists profiled in the book and the only woman.)

Of Detroit, Hughes was quoted as saying, "Harlem used to be the Negro Cultural Center of America. If Detroit has not already become so, it's well on its way to becoming it."

Woodson was certain the world was about to open to her too. "Once I finished my undergrad and graduate school I thought, 'Oh, Shirley, what a perfect moment. You're going to be the first Black woman artist in the world,' I told myself."

But the art world didn't welcome Woodson in the way her education had led her to expect. In her art history classes and books, Woodson had never "seen anyone like myself. So, I had to be the *first*," she says with a hint of sarcasm aimed at the narrowness of her arts education.

She and many other Black artists of the era may as well have been newly descended Martians, undeniably visible but uninvited. "We were out here expressing ourselves, making great work as Black artists, but no one understood the expression because white gallerists didn't have to," Woodson recalls. "In their totality they were it. They hadn't seen us in the books either, and we really didn't know how poorly we'd been prepared for the world outside of a studio. Anything about presenting your work to someone who's never seen it, we didn't have that knowledge."

She adds: "No matter what we showed of ourselves, they weren't going to take any of it because we were not white people. I thought art was about truth and beauty. That world quickly showed me, if we wanted to be in it, we'd have to do everything on our own."

Woodson wasted no time in drawing a new path for herself, thanks to encounters with two key people just as her career was starting. Taylor, the Black art historian and educator, was one. Her launch of a seminal Detroit gallery, Arts Extended, included a job invite for Woodson who was juggling

A close detail from Shirley's painting *Joy, Grief and the Artist*, based on the photograph opposite.

Shirley and her sons Khari (left) and Senghor at the Amherstburg Freedom Museum (Amherstburg, Ontario) in the mid '80s.

her teacher's certification requirements with working part-time as a substitute teacher. "I was suddenly in a professional environment as a Black artist surrounded by other Black artists. It was a moment to be cherished. I can still run through the names."

Woodson's first solo show was there, a major step since Woodson had been using her parents' home as a studio and quasi-gallery space. Woodson went on to be Taylor's first curator at Arts Extended, from 1965 to 1972. Woodson also taught art classes at the gallery.

"One of the reasons I'm proud to have so much of Shirley's work in my collection is that I know the spirit that has driven her for so many years. I saw its start," said Taylor. "She's always had a great painter's eye, but she has an even better eye for creating opportunity for others. She cares and because she does, Shirley Woodson's art has never been just about Shirley Woodson. I love her in my life because of that; she keeps culture and art moving together."

Taylor's assessment is one widely shared.

"One of the things I've always admired about Shirley's work, and I hear from others, too, is that it comes from a great foundation in art history," says Sherry Washington, a private art gallerist and broker who says she has sold hundreds of Woodson paintings since the 1980s. "When Shirley puts down paint or ink, she knows the history of each brush stroke and technique. She also knows the history and cultural tradition that she's painting from as a Black woman artist. And she's not afraid to make it come alive with colors that show how vibrant and joyful the culture is."

Spend any time talking to Woodson about her career's major turning points, and soon enough the conversation swings toward the second central figure in her life, a man with a special book in his hand, and an eye for her paintings. The man was Edsel Reid, a New York–based art collector, student of Black art and a dear friend of her brother, Curtis.

Reid, a native of Inkster, Michigan, was 25 and four years younger than his future bride. Those who knew the couple speak of their union with the highest admiration. "A beautiful Black love story," friends say. Together, they welcomed two sons, Khari and Senghor, and were married for 33 years before Reid died in 2000.

Rooted in Bold

The story starts in 1965 — of course, with art.

Reid was in town collecting work for an upcoming exhibition. During the trip, he decided to drop by his old friend's apartment. A watercolor on the living room wall caught his eye. Immediately, he asked Curtis for details about the artist.

"My brother called and said a friend of his was interested in my work and wanted to see more before he left town," Woodson says. "When he came to my parents' house for the appointment, he started talking, and I realized he knew a lot about art including art history, which was unusual."

Reid purchased four paintings that day.

He also declared to Woodson: "I think I want the whole package."

A near-instant long-distance relationship took off. At the time, Woodson was eager to shed some of the heavy influence of German expressionism that had been foisted upon her during her graduate art student days at Wayne State University. She was hungry for independence and a sense of experimentation in her work similar to what she admired in the work of artists such as Larry Rivers, Milton Avery and Robert Rauschenberg.

Woodson's curiosity and discipline were soon rewarded with a 1966 monthlong fellowship at the prestigious MacDowell colony in New Hampshire. It was January, brutally cold and snowy. Woodson was nonetheless enchanted. "The work I was doing at MacDowell, I hadn't done anything like it anywhere else. I wasn't a student any longer. I wanted to create more light in my work by doing things like working with silver and metallic papers. It was just this wonderful time of exploring and great change."

Reid was a proud supporter. He was also in love. To see the emergence of her new creative direction and to keep Woodson close, he made weekend trips from New York. In 1967, Woodson and Reid grew even closer. They married that summer, a month before the Detroit uprising. For Woodson, the city's uprising coincided with a personal cultural awakening and a conscious artistic shift ignited by Reid's knowledge of art, particularly Black art. "Art brought us together and it changed a lot of my perspectives."

As a birthday gift to his wife, Reid inscribed

Shirley and Edsel Reid in Stratford, Ontario.

Shirley and Edsel with their sons Senghor (in arms) and Khari, 1976.

25

Shirley and Edsel in front of Dudley Randall's home, April 1969.

a now treasured copy of *American Negro Art* by Cedric Dover, a book that he adored. "I said, 'What kind of art is Negro art?'" Woodson says. "It was the start of me discovering so many names and timelines involving Black people and our contribution to art that I'd missed."

The painter had found a life partner and a life purpose well beyond the studio. In 1974 she co-founded the Michigan chapter of the National Conference of Artists (NCA). Suddenly, Woodson had a way of correcting her miseducation as a Black artist while strengthening the knowledge of like-minded Black art creators and enthusiasts.

"I had been taught to believe that art was about truth and beauty," she says. "Once the real world showed me how different the truth was, I wanted others to know too because it was clear that white people, if they knew at all, were not going to tell us about the history or how to even present ourselves as artists."

Founded in 1959, the conference is the nation's oldest arts organization focused on nurturing, developing and promoting opportunities for Black visual artists. With a network across the country, NCA also connects artists to educators, historians, critics, collectors, curators, and gallery owners. Woodson, who retired from public education in 2008, sits on the NCA's executive board and continues to lead the Michigan chapter as its president.

Many artists view NCA's Detroit gallery, currently a space inside the Northwest Activity Center, as a neighborhood hub for creative connection and resources.

When mixed media artist and community art teacher Halima Afi Cassells decided to leave Brooklyn, New York, in 2008 and bring her practice back home to Detroit, Woodson and the NCA were the first places she found support—and work.

"So many of us have benefited from Shirley being this shining example of simply following her heart," says Cassells, who spent six years working with NCA Michigan as a youth arts facilitator and leading mural projects.

"Shirley's heart is why we have an institution that provides a grounding, and space, and knowledge about what it means to be an artist, how you critique and sell and grow. When you look at what she's done, it speaks about how you honor tradition and how you

Shirley with Edsel Reid and their son Khari.

Shirley discussing her works at Detroit's Norwest Gallery as her son, painter Senghor Reid, looks on.

27

Dr. Cledie Taylor and Shirley at Arts Extended Gallery, September 2017.

Shirley, art educator and curator Dr. Cledie Taylor and gallerist Dell Pryor share center stage at the Detroit Institute of Arts in 2019 for a lecture on their contributions to the city's arts community. The trio is known across Detroit as the grande dames of Black art.

continue to stoke the creative fire for all ages so that the community has a lasting entry point."

Kimberly Trent, an avid art collector, is thrilled to have a Woodson painting hanging on her wall. She owns a few works by Woodson's son Senghor as well. Yet the greater delight, says Trent, is having experienced first-hand Woodson's infectious drive and sense of purpose. Trent is a past member of NCA's board of trustees. "We're really blessed that she chose to stay in Detroit," says Trent, who is the deputy director — prosperity for the Michigan Department of Labor and Economic Opportunity.

"Shirley's a true guardian of the culture; someone who genuinely loves exposing people to the talent of our community, who wants to see it thrive, and someone who believes it can emanate from spaces that aren't traditional. You walk through the halls of the Northwest Activity Center and there's beauty there because of Shirley. You want to see people who give of themselves like that, someone who literally nurtures community, honored."

While the tributes surrounding his mother's Kresge Eminent Artist selection are a joy to witness, Khari Reid, Woodson's oldest son, is more thrilled imagining how loudly his father would be celebrating the news and curating Detroit's embrace of his wife.

"He supported her mightily and wanted other people to see the brilliance that he saw," says Reid, whose 10-year-old son Dayton is Woodson's only grandchild. "Growing up, I watched them and the way he cared about her work and encouraged her to push boundaries as much as she could," says Khari, an academic intervention specialist for Detroit Public Schools Community District.

"I know my father would be enjoying this moment, probably more than my mother."

Woodson agrees. For the first time, she has a moment and a reason to take a look backward, to measure her life's impact, and to plot its next chapters. The spectacle of her Kresge selection, the sudden interest from news media and the nonstop calls from supporters and friends have left Woodson more overwhelmed than the accompanying no-strings-attached $50,000 prize. "I think everyone wants, at some point, to see their work celebrated," Woodson says. "I don't think anyone sets out to be an eminent artist. You do the work and over time you hope it carries itself in such a way that it creates enjoyment and fulfillment."

But, Woodson says, "When it suddenly happens at this scale, it's a lot to take in at once. If your work has been about something of importance to you, it's like getting to make those connections for yourself all over again."

Notably, Woodson's Eminent Artist selection coincided with an invitation from the Detroit Artists Market for a major 2021 solo exhibition. Shortly after she accepted, a solo invite from Detroit's historic Scarab Club followed, yet another sign of the widespread embrace of Woodson over the years.

That the wave of attention and accolades emerged in the midst of social and racial unrest surpassing her experience of the 1950s and 1960s, adds to the specialness of the award, she says. "It's scary and some days it's exciting to think of the possibilities that could come from this time."

At least three days a week, Woodson puts in eight hours or more in her studio. Her studio time is often determined by Khari's insistence on chauffeuring her as a pandemic precaution. "My mother has worked too hard for me to let her risk herself."

When she is at the studio, Woodson's laser-like focus is partly because she intends to to cover the walls for both of her 2021 exhibitions with new works. In a studio filled with hundreds of paintings, she could understandably pull from the past.

Instead, she is facing each blank canvas with a vigor that she says comes from discipline and longevity. "The artist is always confronted with the next step. You learn to see every step of the process as a question: What can I share with people? What do I still have to say?"

She adds, "I'm listening and waiting."

Nichole M. Christian is a writer and veteran journalist. She is co-author of *Canvas Detroit*. Her writing also appears in *Portraits 9/11/01: The Collected Portraits of Grief* from *The New York Times*, the online arts journal *Essay'd*, *A Detroit Anthology*, and *Dear Dad: Reflections on Fatherhood*. She was creative director, editor and lead writer of *Wonder and Flow*, the monograph honoring 2020 Kresge Eminent Artist Marie Woo, and of *A Life Speaks*, the monograph honoring 2019 Kresge Eminent Artist Gloria House.

Shirley and the late Gilda Snowden, a long-time protégé and friend, share a moment.

Shirley talks about her work with fellow Detroit painter Priscilla A. Phifer.

29

IN THE TRADITION

Shirley Woodson does not shout as a painter or person. She does not overly prescribe meaning to the choices in her works. Shirley Woodson imagines. She creates, and she trusts in the strength of the traditions that have shaped and sharpened her—Black art, Black culture, Black faith—to lead viewers to their own understanding and connections.

"Whether Jacob Lawrence paints it, or Bob Thompson paints it, or Archibald Motley paints it; whether Augusta Savage sculpts it—it is within our experience," says Woodson. "We have an iconography of kings and queens."

Though Shirley the painter and art historian knows more than she'll ever tell, those who know and have studied her journey on the canvas and beyond say Woodson's works are always saying something: more. The late Gilda Snowden, an acclaimed painter and arts educator, whose legacy is celebrated annually through Kresge-funded Gilda Awards for risk-taking emerging artists, once said this of her mentor: "Shirley deftly unites color, myths, historical references with a little bit of magic into works that are glorious renditions of what life could be and should be."

In that spirit, six artists similarly close to Woodson—painters, curators, art historians and creative protégés—were invited to choose a favorite work as a lens on her expansive legacy as a Black artist, culture keeper and waymaker.

Bold colors, they say, don't begin to tell the whole or the heart of Shirley Woodson.

— **NICHOLE CHRISTIAN**

Shirley with her painting *Figure on the Porch*, 1964, oil on linen, 44 × 50 in.

Her Eye Watches

Allie McGhee

Shirley is a terrific artist. You know that instantly. When you come upon a Shirley Woodson there's no denying her signature palettes that vibrate with such intensity.

As a painter, and colorist myself, and someone who's known Shirley for about 60 years, I'm still amazed. Her work is a sort of bridge between abstract and impressionism. You can see figurative forms that she activates through shapes and rich colors to become representations of many approaches to painting. Anyone who has the opportunity should take the time to see a Shirley Woodson, how she relates it all with such fulfillment for herself and the viewer.

But when you're looking at her work it's important to realize there's much more to what you're seeing. Really, her paintings are like coming in on a movie and there's only five minutes left. You have no idea what's there if you don't know how it all evolved together with her life.

Recently, I came upon a painting of Shirley's that I'd never seen. I received a book about the Detroit artist Harold Neal. I thought it was great to see that we both have work in the book. But this particular piece of Shirley's blew me away: *Martha's Vandellas*. Man, is it something! I had to get a better look. There's the obvious experience of color. But then you see that there is an Egyptian Osiris eye watching over.

The eye is communicating. It shows the power and beauty of research by Black artists so that the substance being talked and painted about is based on history. In the '60s, a lot of us went from painting about the pain of Black people in the United States to higher ground, to times in Africa and specifically in Egypt when we were viewed as mathematicians, architects— people with a rich history who we could enjoy and feel good about. The Osiris eye is a pictorial reminder. People don't realize how much research artists do before we create a visual experience that's based on facts, truth, spirituality, science—on so many unspoken things. As a viewer you don't have to have all of that to enjoy the work, but it's so much better when you do.

The eye in this particular work is also powerful because Shirley is really saying something about who she is and who she's been all these years, not just as a painter. We all came from a period in the '60s where there was little to no opportunity to expose our work to the community. Shirley was the link. She had the connections to museums and galleries and she unselfishly shared. Whatever she saw out there she came back and shared. No one who is contemporary now, but wasn't around back in the '60s and '70s, could possibly understand what kind of a trailblazing person she's been. She's carried such a load for decades. That's heavy duty when you think about the fact that she was making this brilliant body of work the whole time, even during the lean times. A lot of artists are selfish and desperate to get work out because they have to—not Shirley.

It's something to see the whole picture. Shirley would get us various gigs that not only supplied you with money to keep working; it was always a whole experience and real representation to see that here's an actual living Black person, whoever it might be, that has survived and *is* surviving as an artist—a Black artist. Shirley hoisted so many of us up. Her dedication proved that art is something you *can* do. It's not out of reach for the young student in the city of Detroit.

Shirley is a beauty—still out here making art, still watching over.

Martha's Vandellas
1969
Oil on linen
48 × 48 in.

Allie McGhee is a Detroit-based abstract painter whose works are often influenced by jazz and science. His works are included in the collections at the Detroit Institute of Arts, the St. Louis Museum of Art and The Studio Museum in Harlem. McGhee is an original member of Gallery 7, a groundbreaking Black arts space founded in the 1970s by the late Charles McGee, who was also the inaugural Kresge Eminent Artist in 2008.

Carrying It On

The art works of the Shirley Woodson that I know deserve more than a 17-second view, the median time a person views an artwork exhibited in a museum setting, particularly her painting *Biafra Cries, The Thrill Is Gone*.

The creation date and subject tell us of an artist who is keenly aware of the political, cultural and societal shifts occurring in the newly liberated nations of West Africa. "History, time, vision and the spectacular all have a basis in my painting whether thematic or conceptual," Shirley said in describing her work in the seminal *Gumbo Ya Ya: Anthology of Contemporary African American Women Artists* (New York: Midmarch Arts Press, 1995).

The independence movements across the continent gained the attention of African Americans like Shirley who were at the time connecting parallels between the freedom struggles of the newly formed nations and the Civil Rights Movement in the United States. In 1960, Nigeria declared its independence from Britain. Within five years the new nation's bureaucratic government was infused with corruption at all levels, which created tension between cultural groups. (In their scramble to create colonies, the European powers created African nation states without regard to local and/or cultural alliances.) After pushing off the yoke of British colonialism and achieving independence, Nigeria fell into civil war in 1967. The illusion of national independence was short-lived for Biafra's Igbo people as they were now at war with their "country" men. Yes, the thrill was tragically gone.

Pursuing information about life on the continent, Shirley sought out news stories about the conflict in mainstream and alternative American media outlets. Being *au courant* in Black history and culture, she needed to satisfy her curiosity about issues concerning a contemporary war between African peoples. After researching she completed this canvas in 1970, the year the civil war ended.

In creating *Biafra Cries, The Thrill Is Gone*, Shirley becomes storyteller as she describes the resolve of the Igbo women during the Biafran/Nigerian Civil War. Through visual symbols, she lays out clues about the women's lives. The painting's entry point is the faces of three women. The women, two with facial features and one who is faceless, are resolute in their gaze and dress as they understood the war to be a pogrom, an elongated exercise designed to eliminate the Igbo people and their culture. Projecting staid intention to protect their own, the women are dressed in starched white shirts, which exemplified their modern and progressive thoughts, and solidarity to the fight for Biafra, as they move cautiously carrying small,

PREVIOUS PAGES

Biafra Cries, The Thrill Is Gone (diptych)
1970
Oil on canvas
two canvases, 34 × 56 in. each.

36

Camille Ann Brewer

short-range missiles atop their coiffed, cloth-wrapped heads.

Through a woman's gaze, Shirley provides a window into the lives of Igbo women. It was the mothers, daughters and sisters who maintained the secret night markets under forest canopies to maintain a local economy, dealt with issues of food insecurity and safety for their families, and transported weapons and other goods over enemy lines to support the war effort. "Reference to the historical may be coupled with ideas of familial energy," says Shirley. This is exactly what she brilliantly illustrates in this work, the dignity, principles, strength, bravery and determination of Igbo women who pushed through major struggles to protect and maintain their familial culture.

Yet despite the complexity of her subject matter, *Biafra Cries, The Thrill Is Gone* captures another important truth: Shirley Woodson *knows* visual art. She knows it throughout her entire spiritual being. Shirley is first and foremost a painter trained in the Western tradition of composition building. She knows art history, how to create artwork, and how to present artwork. This bench of knowledge accompanies her hand each time she applies a brush stroke to any canvas.

The compositional structure of *Biafra Cries* tells us of a painter well-versed in design principles, as she uses select methods to pull in and hold her viewer so that they may take more time to "listen" to this chapter of Nigerian history. Shirley uses a gray-scale palette to draw attention to the figures and as a tool to visually push the forms off the canvas' surface so that they occupy space with the viewer. She employs complementary colors to further define and give dimension to the figures, while also creating a visual tension between the forms as they move closely together.

The composition is a diptych canvas built on a one-third, two-thirds ratio, which is a classic method used to create aesthetic positions for primary elements in a painting. Woodson engages the same ratio placing the three figures vertically like sequential keys across the picture plane. This alignment indicates that the women are traveling as a unit. However, the painter carefully pays attention to define each figure as a distinct character with a greater story. The painting beckons and holds our attention, and once the story is revealed, the image sears into one's memory.

In *Biafra Cries, The Thrill Is Gone*, we are told of an African history, and a visionary artist, we must never forget.

Camille Ann Brewer is the principal of Erik Van Wert Dye Works, a textile design business based in Detroit. Brewer earned a Bachelor of Fine Arts from California College of the Arts and a Master of Fine Arts from the University of Michigan. Brewer also earned a Master of Library and Information Science from Valdosta State University in Georgia. She lives in Detroit.

Evening Glow
2012
Collage
11 × 14 in.

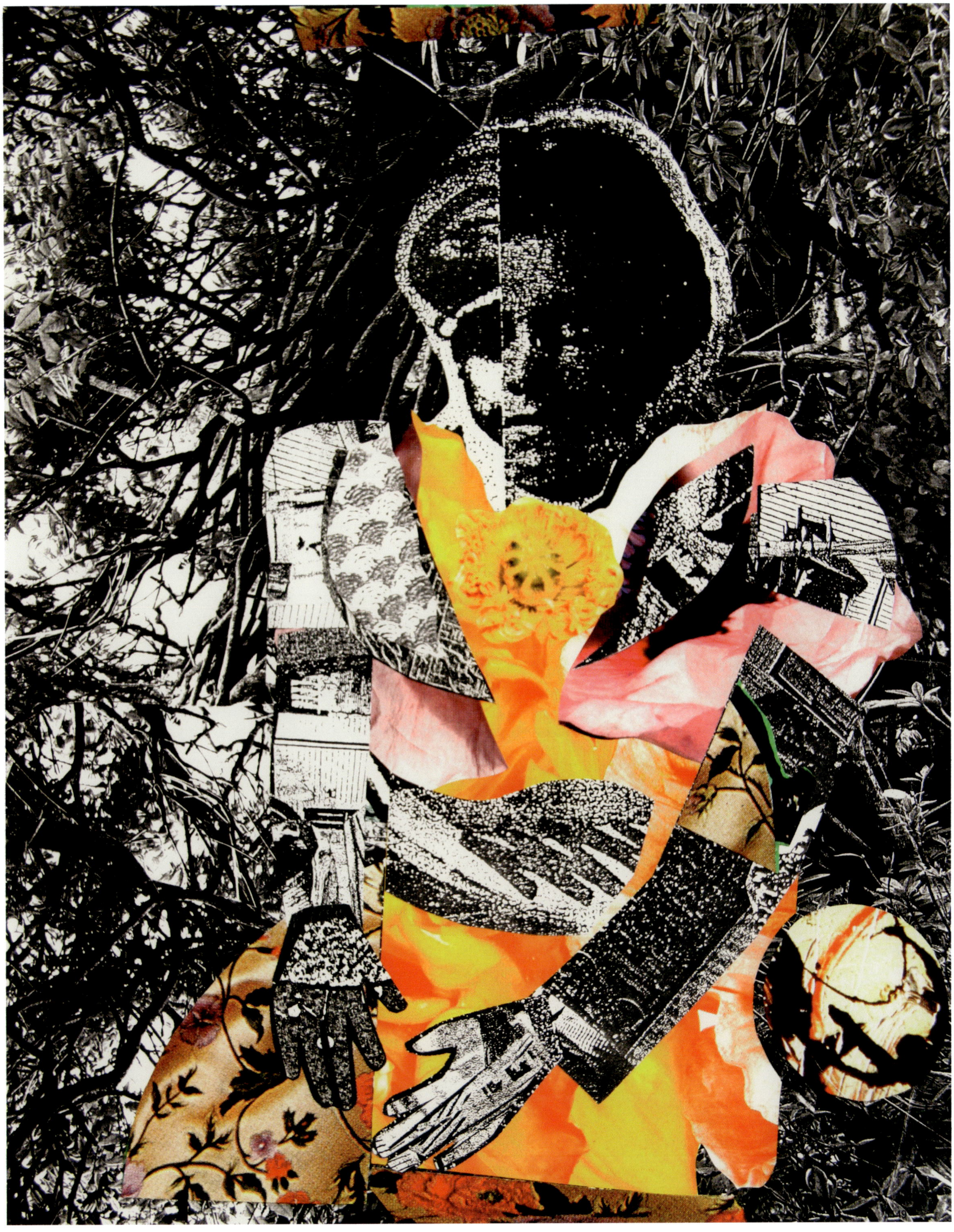

The Giver

It is impossible to look at any work by Shirley Woodson, a painting or a collage, and not think about the colors first. They're overwhelming. She's bold about how she uses colors and her choices are always beautiful.

But as far as I'm concerned, Shirley's generosity as an artist, her way of using color to celebrate and educate, and to depict the joy, beauty and the power of African American culture is what makes her one of the greatest African American women artists that we have. Shirley is purposeful in her depiction of Black women and the Black family in her work. I've always appreciated that. The intense colors are her way of showing how much she understands and cares about the importance of placing African American heritage and strength at the center and being unapologetic about the choice.

You see it over and over in her work because the colors also represent who Shirley is as a person, not just as an artist. Family and community and Black womanhood are what she draws from as a foundation and what she invites others to appreciate with her. One of the first collections of her works that I ever showed at the Dell Pryor Gallery was a series of collages about her family and her ancestral home. I was instantly impressed by how committed she was to her themes and to the history. Shirley is steadfast about showing these elements in her work and it's one of the ways she's made a huge contribution to the culture through art. In her collages and stories, she's telling us stories. In some of her works like *Evening Glow*, you see women whose eyes appear to be looking right at you, daring you to look away.

Shirley cares about drawing people closer. She connects artists who on their own might not immediately see different opportunities for their work. There's no separation in her work or her life. When I first decided I wanted to open my own African American art gallery in the late 1980s, Shirley was the person I went to. At that time, Shirley Woodson was the only person with a gallery space still completely dedicated to supporting African American artists.

She could've been discouraging, but she immediately gave me encouragement and became most helpful to me. She saw the benefit as an artist and as someone uplifting other African American artists, to having another African American woman-owned gallery space open in the city. I could call on her at any time, any hour; I still can because of her generosity of spirit. The vibrancy you see in her work is also who she is in the city and in the lives of so many artists. In the same way you see intricate layers in her collage work, there are so many layers to the ways Shirley has woven together this rich multigenerational community of African American artists.

Before I opened my gallery, I was a commercial and residential interior designer. I was focused on trying to get the works of African American artists on the walls in corporations and doctors' offices and local businesses. A lot of it involved me commissioning artists to create original works. It helped that I knew a lot of mid-career artists in the city at the time.

But when I opened the gallery, it was Shirley who helped me see all the young talent on the horizon in Detroit. She recommended and introduced me to all of these young and emerging artists whose

PREVIOUS PAGE
Evening Glow
2012
Collage
11 × 14 in.

Dell Pryor

work and careers she was connected to because she had opened the National Conference of Artists' gallery here. She would literally bring new young artists to the gallery. I don't think anyone can count how many artists Shirley has in some way been instrumental in helping become connected to the gallery circuit including getting them exposure in reputable galleries.

She's really built a vibrant community, and she's given it the same careful attention that makes you notice what she creates as an artist. You can't ignore the contributions she's made with her art and to art including a son, Senghor, who is also one of our finest artists. It just warms my heart that I've been able to show their work together. I'm even happier because now the entire city—and so many others I hope—has a reason to stand back and look at how total this one woman's contributions have been down through the years before there ever was a Kresge Eminent Artist award, and even still to this day.

The Shirley Woodson story just goes on and on and on.

Shirley and Dell Pryor at the Detroit Artists Market, April 2017.

Dell Pryor is the founder and director of the Dell Pryor Gallery, a space celebrated for more than 30 years of showcasing new, national and established Detroit artists. Pryor most recently curated *A Common Thread, 2020*, in partnership with the Detroit Artists Market. She was a member of the 2021 Kresge Eminent Artist selection panel.

We Were on the Island
2008
Collage
8 × 11 in.

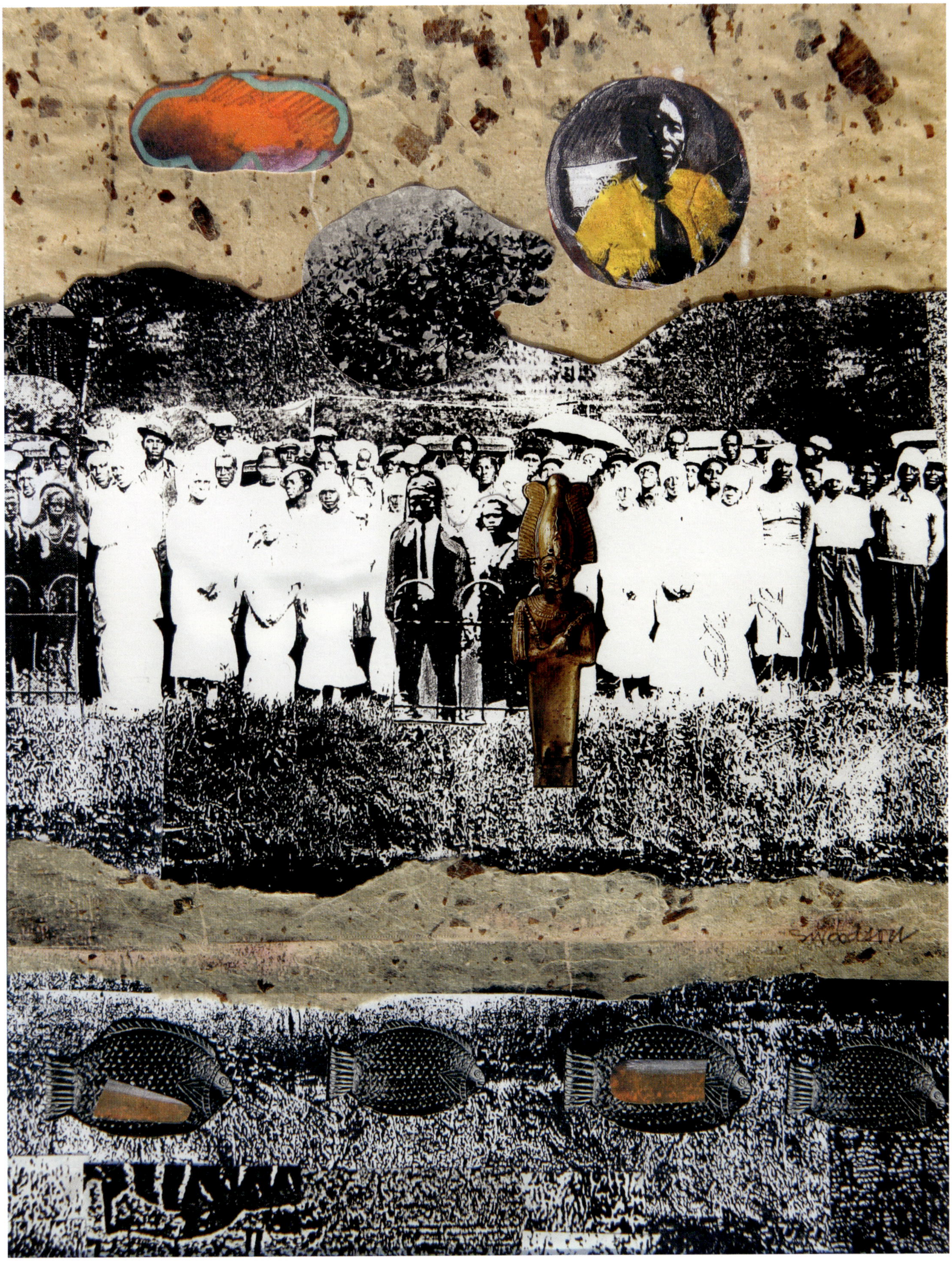

Orbiting Shirley

I don't remember when I first met Shirley Woodson. It's as if I've known her most of my life. In truth, I met her son Senghor Reid first. Senghor and I were students at the University of Michigan School of Art & Design (now the Stamps School of Art & Design). He was pursuing a Bachelor of Fine Arts, and I was pursuing a Master of Fine Arts in painting. We graduated in 1999.

While attending U-M, I was introduced to Detroit, and ultimately ushered into Shirley's world by my professor Nancy Thayer, who challenged students to find an artist like themselves. She was pretty direct: "If you are a white male, find a white male artist. If you're a Black female, find a Black female artist." I was new to the area so she recommended I meet the artist Gilda Snowden who had a studio in the same building as she did.

Thayer connected us and I headed to Detroit (this must've been 1997 or 1998) with my 8mm video camera and no clue that this encounter would be one of the greatest of my artistic life. If you knew Gilda, you would say the same. It wasn't long before I realized that if you knew Gilda, you would soon know Shirley, women who were each paving the way for more Black artists in Detroit.

In 2001, I made the leap and moved to Detroit. I made my way around galleries and neighborhoods including the National Conference of Artists (NCA) space where I got to know Shirley more. She spoke about balancing family and career and knowing that there are seasons for everything in one's life. It was not strange to see her grandson at NCA drawing or just hanging with his grandmother. I loved it. In 2003, I got married and started a family and an after-school arts, academic and leadership program in my neighborhood, following much in the ways of Shirley.

Fast forward to 2012, the year I formed Live Coal Gallery. It was an absolute honor to exhibit Shirley's collage work during my gallery's beginning. At the time, I had four children and worked on and off as an artist-in-residence teaching art in Detroit Public Schools. As an artist-mom-gallerist-educator, someone like Shirley became a friend, a parent figure, a peer and a mentor all at once. Shirley was something to behold. She was never anxious, and when I would tell her what was happening in my life, she always had something timely and inspiring to say. Family was almost never far from our conversations.

A few months prior to opening Live Coal, Shirley had a solo NCA show called *On Angel Wing: Collages 2002–2012*. Though I couldn't be there, I am forever thankful to our mutual friend Gilda for recording the opening and capturing the beauty of Shirley's collage works. The subject that dominates her collages are photographs of her family members. Shirley believes the subject of family is one that viewers can connect with. She places the figures in idyllic settings because that is how her family history was presented to her. "Families are so important," she says. "They make us who we are."

One of my favorite pieces

PREVIOUS PAGE

We Were On the Island

2002

Collage

8 × 11 in.

44

Yvette Rock

from that show is called *We Were on the Island, 2008*. The scene is a baptism. The piece is divided into four horizontal segments, with the middle ground being the largest. The top of the piece utilizes some kind of cream-colored handmade paper pressed with bark. Collaged on top of this "sky" are two cutouts—one of an orange-colored cloud form that is informally outlined in a teal color and the other a cutout in the shape of a circle featuring a portrait of a woman. This woman, who is floating and hovering above the collage, reminds me of a mother who has gone on to the eternal and is witnessing the actions of her family members down below, and perhaps even overseeing the baptism. In the middle ground we see a crowd of witnesses standing along a grassy field that is beside a collaged image of what appears to be mud. Just below that we see four fish swimming in a row inside what appears to be a river. The scene is dramatic.

The collage's central figure is a bronze-colored sarcophagus standing in front of the crowd on the grassy field. Since a baptism is taking place, we can suspect that the sarcophagus is about to be immersed in the water. The symbolism is striking. Baptisms symbolize a person immersing themselves in water in order to "die to themselves" and "be reborn." A sarcophagus holds a once living person who is now dead.

Perhaps the work is alluding to the ancient people being immersed in a new culture and able to come back to life. The title, *We Were on the Island*, is peculiar as well. Does Shirley want us to think about nationalism or colonialism? Should we reflect on the history of Black people who have been scattered on so many islands whilst under the rule of foreign governments, yet as resilient people able to be reborn and come back to life? Will we conform like the fish or will we change the course of our history?

The great cloud of witnesses, and, in this case, the main female figure hovering above the drama, quietly yet resolutely look at us and call us to ponder these questions; they call us to ponder our place, our belonging and our own life journey just as Shirley Woodson has.

Shirley poses for a selfie with her oldest son Khari, and his son, Dayton Reid, an 11-year-old competitive golfer and artist.

Yvette Rock received a BFA from Cooper Union in 1997 and an MFA in painting from the University of Michigan in 1999, where she was also a visiting scholar and founder of Detroit Connection, a program created to build collaborations between the university and Detroit schools and organizations. Rock is a longtime artist-in-residence with InsideOut Literary Arts Project. In 2018, she founded The RED, a children's community-based art museum in Detroit. She is also the founder of Bezalel Project, an after-school program, and the mobile Live Coal Gallery. Rock is a 2019 Facing Change: Documenting Detroit fellow.

Re-entry
2014–2020
Acrylic on canvas
40 × 40 in.

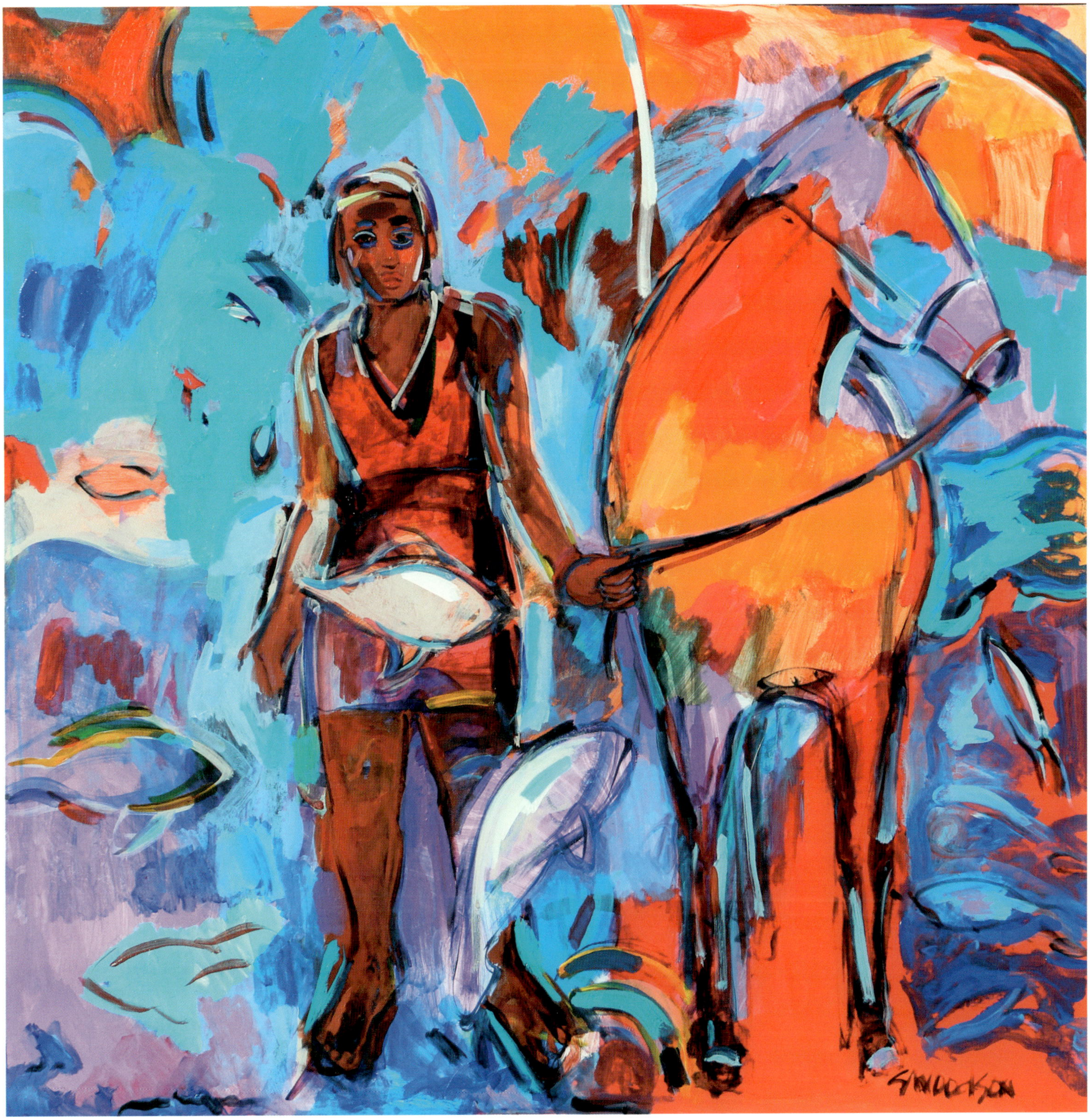

Inheritance

I've been a student of the works and ways of Shirley Woodson's art for more years than I can count, but one painting has always stood out. *Re-entry* is a very spiritual painting, defining the significant role of the matriarch, the one that has the responsibility to empower communities and their people. The matriarch is the activist and the social change agent.

In *Re-entry*, the Black woman stands calmly amidst any forceful adversary and the strongest elements such as water, wind, and heat. Her stance is brawny. This painting defines the significant role of the empowered Black woman as she is grounded in an intellect and strength. She births the transformation of countless generations. She is masterful in aiding her people. Spurred by spirituality, she nurtures and brings forth abundant life, wealth and power.

The figure in the painting is leading a horse emerging from the waters with sunlight shining down from each corner. The horse represents wealth and power. His head is turned to make sure he's aware of what is coming. While the horse is looking off to the side to protect the woman, she is guiding him while also giving him enough leeway so that he can perform his duty. The images of fish moving throughout the painting represent potency and creativity. The water is the source of purification and life. The colors, red in its superiority, reflect all the symbols that are present in many African cultures.

The painting is filled with symbolic yet recognizable images such as the female figure, the horse and the fish. The background is abstracted with vibrant colors such as cerulean blue, cadmium yellow, crimson red, and other mixed hues, which are symbolic in their own right, as they energetically sweep across each crest. The whirlwind of brushstrokes and carefully layered primary and secondary colors seems to obscure hidden symbols and messages.

In these choices, Woodson provides the viewer with coded language, a visual vocabulary to be deciphered and understood by the matriarch's community. This is prevalent in the art and objects used in African and African American cultures. Those who know, *know*.

Shirley Woodson, a master painter, scholar of her culture, and educator, shows that she surely knows. She creates artwork rooted in African principles, symbolism and traditions. As she creates, she educates. Taking on the role of an African American visual storyteller, Shirley's approach encourages the viewer to travel beyond what the eye perceives. She exposes the eyes and mind to challenge what is known and reveal what is unknown with the utmost seriousness and care.

Re-entry reminds me of my first encounter with Shirley in 1998. I was a young art student at the College for Creative Studies. I had an assignment to interview an artist that was like me, a Black woman painter. I could think of only

PREVIOUS PAGE

Re-entry

2014–2020

Acrylic on canvas

40 × 40 in.

Jocelyn Rainey

one: Gilda Snowden. But the instructor said that Professor Snowden was off limits. Gilda suggested that I interview an artist named Shirley Woodson who was at that time the director of the fine arts department for Detroit Public Schools. I made an appointment to meet with her and we spoke for a long time. I attempted to grasp as much information as possible. When my recorder broke in the middle of our conversation, I apologized. Shirley was so gracious. She told me not to worry; that we could stay as long as I needed.

The last question I asked her was, "What do you do when you have artist's block?"

I've never forgotten her answer: "African American artists don't have time for artist's block. If you cannot finish a painting, that means that you need more information. So, during that time you should be looking at artwork, reading about art, listening to music or writing. You need to be doing things that will assist you in taking your creativity to the next level."

That explanation changed my life and approach as an artist. I can proudly say that with those words Shirley Woodson ignited my transition from student to professional.

As a professional, I continued to study her art and her transforming leadership skills. I saw a woman artist, Black like me, who believed in the power of pushing yourself to expand your thoughts and to never remain where you started. To learn from Shirley Woodson is to learn to investigate the unknown and be comfortable with the discoveries made in the process.

Early in my art career, I was so proud of this one acrylic painting. I was exploring a unique new style of painting. I asked Shirley to critique my artwork. She looked over the painting in her careful way, studying every stroke as if she could see through my thoughts. She paused and said, "You need to create a hundred of these paintings then you will find the answer you seek."

Although I was a little disappointed in the answer, I went and created over a hundred paintings, realizing with each one that Shirley Woodson, an accomplished Black woman painter and historian, had given me, an aspiring young Black woman artist, a true inheritance, a way to build and grow. I am still proudly drawing on her wisdom.

Shirley, Jocelyn Rainey and Leslie Graves at the National Conference of Artists Art Party, October 2018.

Jocelyn Rainey is currently a PhD candidate; her dissertation is focused on the artwork of Gilda Snowden and Shirley Woodson. She received a BFA from the College for Creative Studies and an MA in painting from Wayne State University in Detroit. Her studies included painting, sculpture and mixed media. Rainey's work may be found in many public and private collections, including Blue Cross/Blue Shield of Michigan, TCF Center, Coleman A. Young Municipal Center, Detroit Police Department Headquarters, Comerica Park, Detroit Children's Museum, and Detroit Public Schools Community District. Recent solo exhibitions include *Art of Jocelyn Rainey, an installation of 1001 paintings* at the G.R. N'namdi Center for Contemporary Art; sculptural assemblages using found objects and denim at the College for Creative Studies; and the *Say It Loud* exhibition at the Charles H. Wright Museum of African American History.

Flight into Egypt No. 1 (detail)
1970
Oil on linen
36 × 48 in.

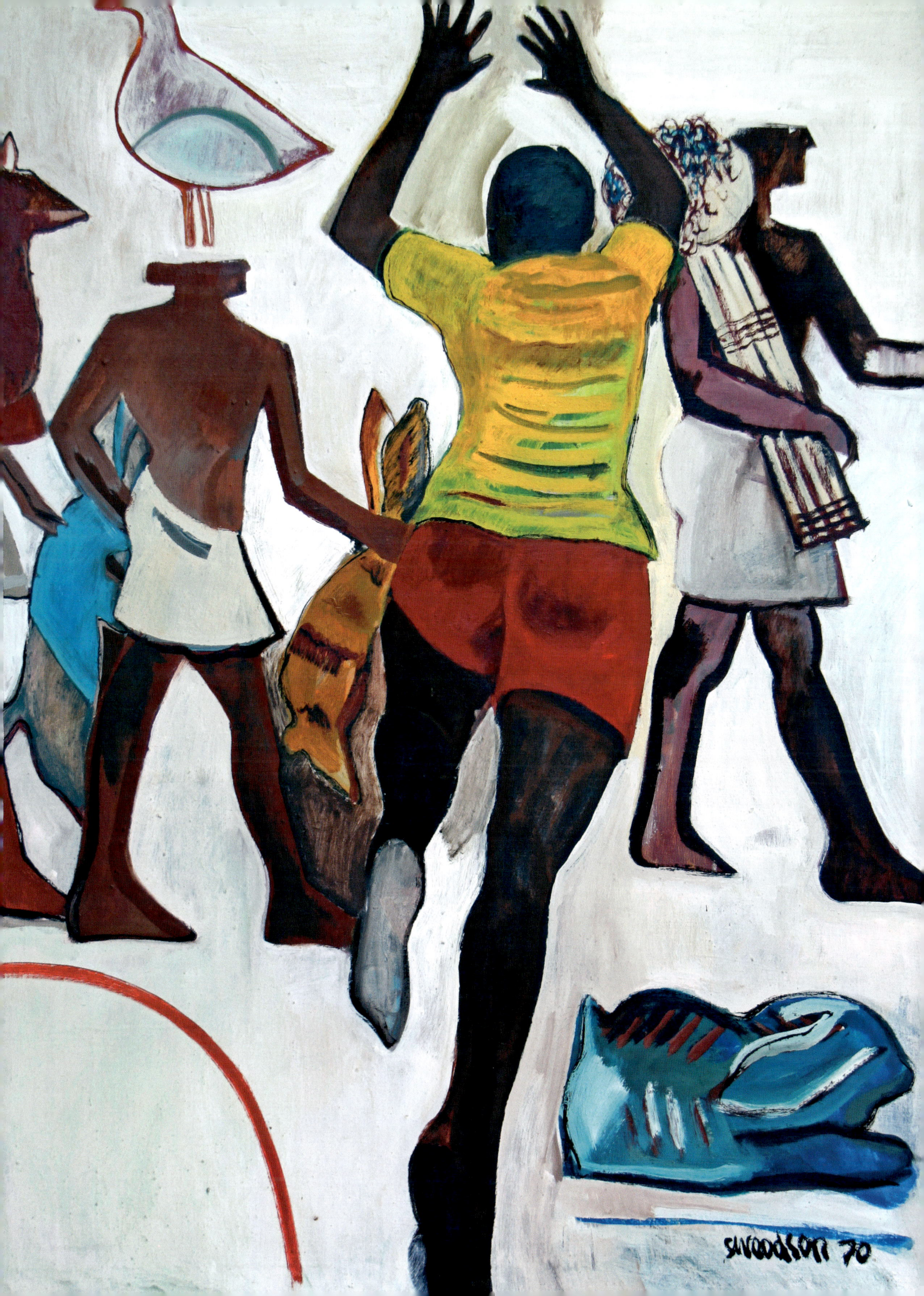
SWoodson 70

A Son Sees Best

As a young boy, I spent a great deal of time at my grandmother Celia's home, a corner house on San Juan in northwest Detroit. Above her bed hung my mother's painting *Flight Into Egypt No.1*. In the painting, a young man appears to be jumping as if he were blocking a volleyball over a net. The boy's back is facing the viewer, with both arms raised, and his left knee leads his momentum up and forward. The boy's brightly painted yellow shirt and cherry red shorts make this a playful painting that I always enjoyed seeing whenever I visited my grandmother.

Although this painting, as the marquee work of art in the house, brought me a great deal of comfort, I always wondered about my mother's treatment of the background. I always thought it was a curious pose because the painting is absent any sort of ball or net. Behind the figure of the boy, animals seem to be walking upright alongside human figures who aren't quite human. I always assumed the animals were hares based on the shape of their ears and snubbed short tails. All of the figures are seen in profile as they appear to be walking to the right as though they are in a march or procession. A robust white bird hovers over the figures to the upper left and a crouching blue rabbit rests in the lower right corner of the composition with a horizontal blue line resting atop my mother's signature. A beautiful red arcing line keeps the eye from falling off the canvas in the lower left corner.

The juxtaposition of the seemingly playful figure against a backdrop of a completely unrelated parade of figures forever puzzled me. Where was the volleyball? Where were the children on the other team? And why were they not all on a beach with splashing blue water? What were bunny rabbits doing walking around in the background? Why did my grandmother choose this painting to hang above her bed?

What did Mommy intend for this painting to be? Moreover, what did she intend for this piece to *do*?

As I would learn later, the answers to some of my questions lay a continent away in the choices of Lt. Col. Odumegwu Ojukwu. He declared the secession of three states of Nigeria's southeastern region in late May 1967 under the name the Republic of Biafra. With the blessings and gifts of ammunition from the British government, the Republic of Nigeria declared war on the newly declared republic as fighting broke out in July starting a full-scale civil war. Despite several early victories, Biafran forces quickly began to buckle as Nigeria penetrated the Igbo heartland over the next two years. This conflict, which claimed thousands of military casualties on both sides, crippled the Biafran economy as its oil fields had been seized.

PREVIOUS PAGE
Flight into Egypt No. 1 (detail)
1970
Oil on linen
36 × 48 in.

52

Senghor Reid

The most decisive strategic move made by the Nigerians was to impose a full-scale economic blockade on the Biafran region. It may have been the single most destructive decision made in West African history. Without its primary sources of revenue, the newly formed republic could not afford to import a diversity of food and resources to its people. Local farmers and fishermen were also limited in their ability to provide enough food for millions of people. By the summer of 1968, Igbo mothers began emerging from the deep bush carrying starving children.

By the time Biafra surrendered to Nigeria in early 1970 well over two million people had died from malnutrition.

Once I was finally able and mature enough to ask my mother about this painting, her explanation and deep connections to the continent surprised me. *Flight Into Egypt No. 1* was the first painting my mother completed after the Biafran genocide. She was in a state of shock after so many missionaries and priests stood by as innocent Black people were murdered, persecuted, starved and abandoned as a result of a European-sponsored war on African soil. This was a protest painting. This painting was about humanity or the loss thereof. What I had long thought was just a boy jumping for joy was actually a boy lying on the ground. Dead. My mother used many photographs published in *The New York Times* for this painting and one of them was a bird's-eye view picture of a boy lying in the street after having been murdered.

The economic blockade had stopped the Biafran importation of seafood and fish from Norway. Other meats such as chicken, beef and pork were usually used only for special occasions and were generally very expensive. Thus, millions of civilians suffered from the acute protein deficiency disease known as kwashiorkor. Their diet had been reduced to almost 100 percent starch. This was why my mother decided to paint the background a milky white color.

The figures in the background had come from the tomb of Nebamun, where artists created images of large processions of people carrying agricultural offerings such as hares and wheat to the wealthy Egyptian accountant. Joining this procession after his death, the soul of the Biafran boy was travelling to meet the ancestors in the afterlife.

This painting was about my mother reaching out to the motherland of all civilization through her creative practice, in an effort to reclaim, recodify, and reassimilate the motherland's source energy with purpose and intent. Both the boy and my mother were running to the past for salvation and safety.

At my grandmother's house, I always sat on the floor at the foot of her bed equally mesmerized by the painting and the intricacies of making my own Transformer toy figures using markers, crayons, cardboard, masking tape and tin foil. Looking back, I am so grateful for having had the privilege of creating toys beneath a beautiful painting of a Biafran boy playing volleyball.

Senghor Reid explores the interactions between the human body and the environment, creating visual representations of dreams, memories and traces of human contact with nature. Reid earned a BFA from the University of Michigan in Ann Arbor, a Master of Arts in Teaching from Wayne State University in Detroit and attended the internationally recognized Marathon Program at the New York Studio School of Drawing, Painting and Sculpture in New York. He is currently an artist-in-residence at the Cranbrook Schools in Bloomfield Hills, Michigan, and is a national board certified visual arts educator.

His awards include the 2009 Kresge Arts in Detroit Visual Artist Fellowship and the prestigious ArtServe Michigan Governor's Award for an Emerging Artist. Reid's work has been exhibited in the U.S. and abroad in galleries and museums including the Museum of Contemporary Art Detroit, Kentler International Drawing Space in New York, St. Catharines Museum and Welland Canals Centre in Ontario, Canada, and the Schomburg Center for Research in Black Culture in New York. His work also appears in private, public and corporate art collections.

Senghor Reid
The Ruling Class: Shirley Woodson
2021
3-color serigraph on paper
22 × 30 in.

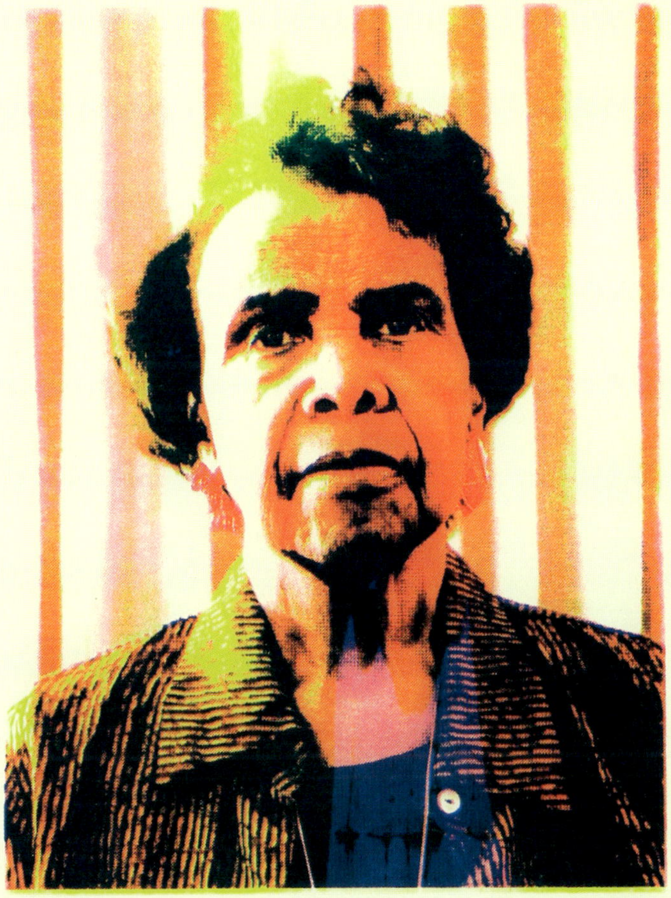

Salon

Curated selections from various themed series Woodson produced, beginning in the 1960s.

Flights, Crossroads and Journeys

Equal parts artist and explorer, Woodson meticulously investigates new roads into familiar concepts such as flight, journeys and crossroads. Woodson is forever willing to see and see again. With the aid of intense colors, she welcomes her viewers to revisit, perhaps even expand, their understanding too.

Flight into Egypt No. 8
2006
Acrylic on canvas
36 × 48 in.

Crossroads at Sea
2006
Acrylic on canvas
30 x 22 in.

Flight into Egypt No. 3
1996
Acrylic on canvas
38½ x 59 in.

Bathers and the Sea

The W in Shirley Woodson's name could easily stand for a lifelong love of water as a force of nature and a source of creative expression. She has painted multiple series that look to the water, including beach gatherings and a homage to the Nile river, as a central subject. "I am intrigued with the challenge of painting water," she says, "its transparency and its translucency."

On the Beach
1959
Oil on canvas
28 × 20 in.

Bathers in Yellow Landscape (detail)
2002
Acrylic on canvas
40 × 30 in.

Four at Sea
2006
Acrylic on canvas
48 × 48 in.

Ancestors Known and Unknown

Shirley Woodson's foray into collages and assemblages began in 1992 with an invitation to participate in *Coast to Coast, A Women of Color National Artists Book Project*. For the project, she collaborated with protégé, friend and fellow painter Gilda Snowden. Their collaboration ignited a love for a new form of expression and an ongoing Woodson series entitled *Ancestors Known and Unknown*.

Through a blend of photo-based collages and assemblages, Woodson found an unexpected portal to explore her family's history. Many of the works in the series are transformed cigar boxes that feature writings and found materials reminiscent of her grandfather's farm in rural Tennessee. "These works somehow help me to call up the memories of the South and the beauty of those places that I've been. Ancestry carries important stories and sources of strength."

Their Names Are On My Lips
2002
Mixed media/collage
13 × 10 in.

Why Do I Delight
1995
Mixed media/collage
8 × 6 × 3 in. (closed)

For Grandmother Rebecca
2003
Mixed media/collage
24 × 18 in.

Ancestors Known

1981

Mixed media/collage

13 × 8.5 × 2 in. (closed)

OPPOSITE

Grandmother with Cloud Cover

2015

Mixed media/collage

10 × 14 in.

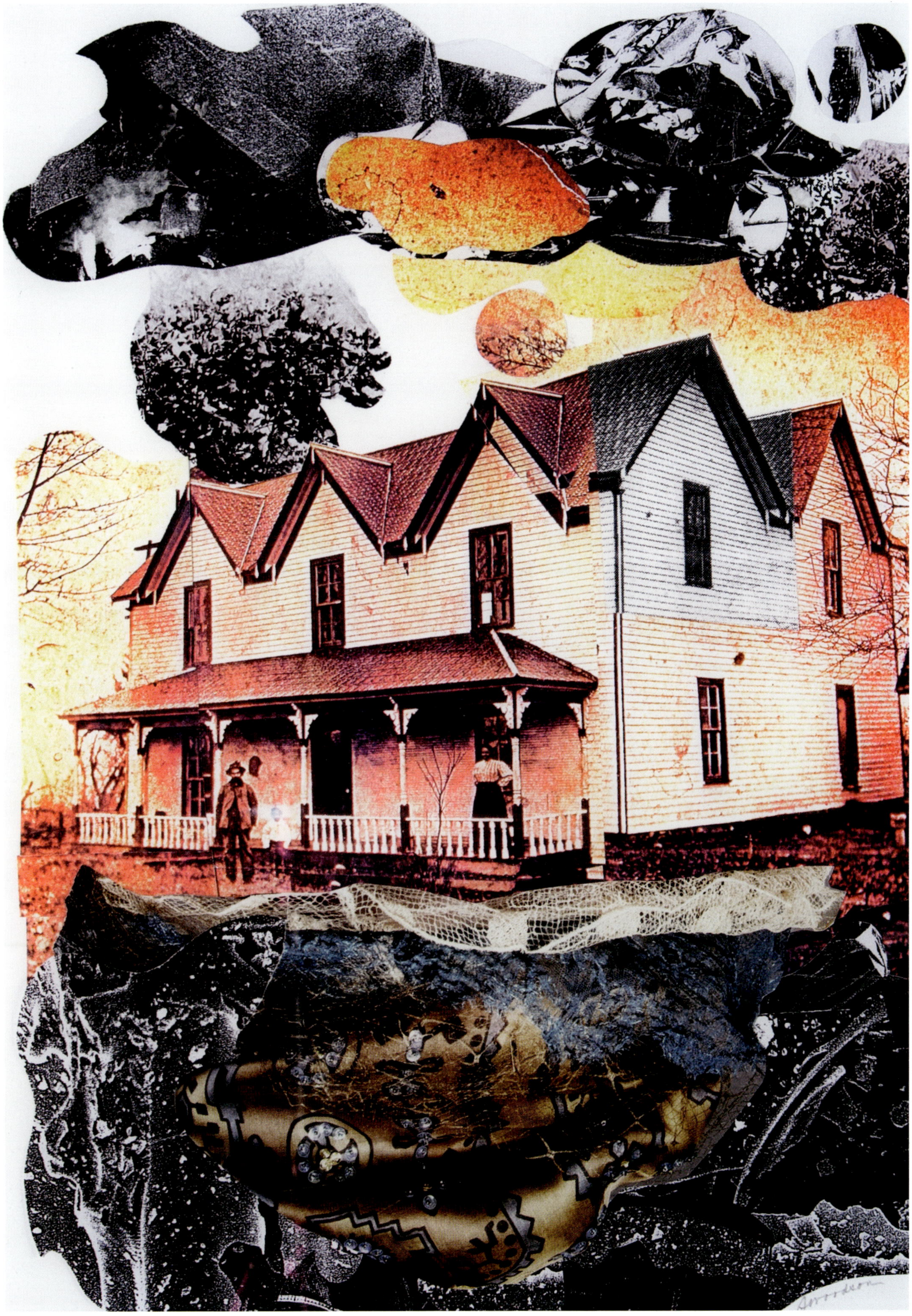

The Painter and the Poet

Only once in Shirley Woodson's life has art ever stopped. The year was 1972. Shirley was in the early stages of one of her life's most important chapters, motherhood. The baby boy she'd given birth to, Khari, had been crowned the pride of the family. But in October of that year, five months before Khari's second birthday, all joy paused. Shirley the mesmerized new mother became the saddened daughter mourning the death of her dear father, Claude. Even now, 49 years later, Woodson does not speak of the moment easily. The words that do emerge arrive coated with a pain that still sounds fresh and an accompanying detail as striking as her work.

"I didn't paint," Woodson recalls as she sits in her studio surrounded by decades and decades of paintings. "For almost two years, I had nothing to say. Whatever ideas and thoughts that would come felt meaningless in the wake of that level of loss for our family." Claude E. Woodson, who was 62 when he died, had been a tower of strength, provision and encouragement for his tight-knit family of four. "It was really the first time death had come so close to me." For the funeral, Woodson the painter attempted to capture her father's legacy in her other favorite art form, words.

> A light beam so strong it defied the natural
> laws and bent around all the harsh corners to find us
> and keep us warm.
> A light stream liquified to bathe us and we knew
>   no thirst.
> A light glow that told us of the sweetness
> of the Motherland.
> A full glow of moon and stars so that night never
>   overtook us.
> An incandescence — brother to the sun — and we
>   became
> children of the SUN
> HE WROTE OUR HISTORY IN LIGHT
> —Shirley Woodson, *For Our Father*, for
>   Claude E. Woodson, October 16, 1972.

Dudley Randall, a legendary poet and publisher, was a great friend of Woodson and joined her in writing a poem to memorialize her father. Randall eventually did something greater. He coaxed Woodson's siphoned creativity back to life by turning to her as a go-to book cover and poster designer for his publishing company, Broadside Press, which he founded in 1965 and operated largely alone from his Detroit home at the height of the Black Arts Movement. Broadside quickly sealed a page in literary history as a vital resource for emerging Black poets and writers, and as a place with a mission that established Black writers wanted to be associated with such as Gwendolyn Brooks, the first Black woman to receive a Pulitzer Prize, and Margaret Walker, who became the first Black woman to receive the preeminent Yale Series of Younger Poets Award. Both Brooks and Walker were published by Broadside. (Broadside Press was also the publishing home of *Blood River*, the first book of poetry written by 2019 Kresge Eminent Artist Dr. Gloria House.)

While Randall, who died in 2000, has been lionized for his work publishing more than 200 Black writers in his time, the work with Woodson, and that of other visual artists, speaks to a respect for creativity in multiple forms, and as a unifying force strong enough to break through barriers, including, in Woodson's case, grief.

After the funeral, Woodson's passion for art making, and her paint brushes, dried up. "The motivation was just gone," she recalled. "But I'd get these wonderful calls from Dudley asking, 'Shirley, how are you?' Then, he'd say, 'I'd like to know if you could do something for me?'" Rarely did Woodson decline Randall's requests, which typically involved helping him create a visual identity for posters, signature broadsides and book covers. "Dudley never assumed," she says. "He always asked you in his deliberate yet kind way."

The creative respect between Randall the publisher and Woodson the painter was an outgrowth of a bond that began several years earlier. When her son was born, Randall wrote a poem to salute Khari's arrival. That same year, the pair collaborated for an exhibition entitled *The Poet and The Painter*. Woodson made paintings in response to

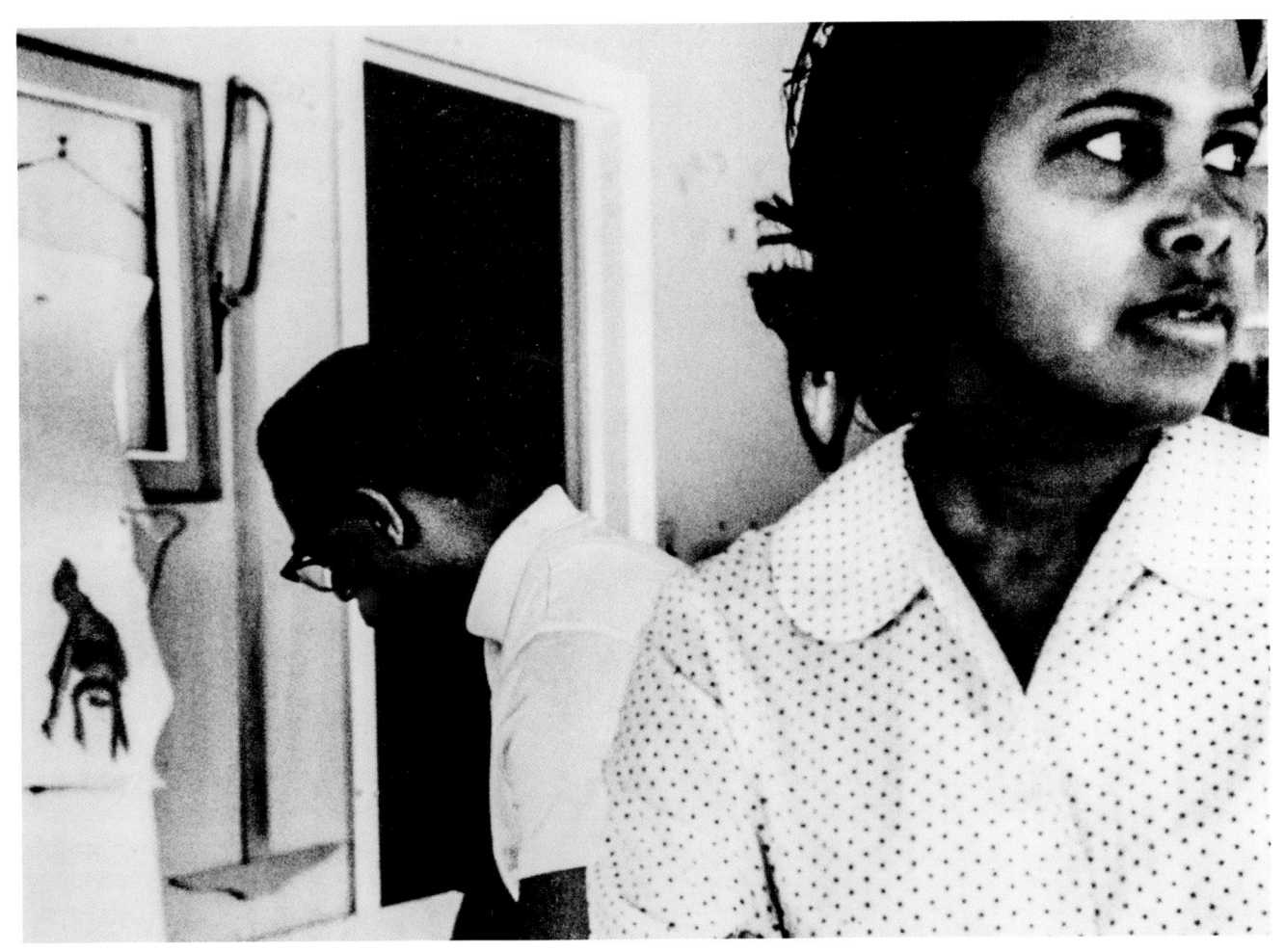

Shirley with Dudley Randall in her home studio, ca. 1970.

Randall's poems. "I was just so in awe of Dudley Randall, and all that he was doing to care for the work of others. It was a very exciting time creatively."

Woodson's designs would help Randall showcase the works of a wide mix of major Black voices, many of whose works continue to this day to be referenced as groundbreaking, including poets such as Sonia Sanchez, June Jordan, Audre Lorde and Randall himself, whose famous *Ballad of Birmingham* she designed for a broadside edition in 1965. The design for that iconic poem was the first work Woodson created for Randall, marking the start of occasional assignments.

To Woodson, the collaboration was more friendship in action and a welcome way to keep some of the grief at bay. During the day she busied herself by continuing to teach art in Highland Park Public Schools. "I really couldn't do anything that required my own expression," she says. "I was happy really just to be busy."

The fact that her designs were part of a history making, and distinctly Black, literary legacy came into view years later. However, her husband, Edsel Reid, predicted the future and told her. "He'd always say, 'This is going to be some of the most important work that you do.' I'd listen, and just say, 'OK. All right.' Anything for Dudley, who was just so honorable. I just wanted to help."

Randall's official biographer, poet Dr. Melba Joyce Boyd, equates Woodson's contributions more closely to art than "help."

"Dudley Randall was a publisher who was also a librarian," she explains. "He insisted that books, and the broadsides — not just the poems — be done at a high artistic level, and in Shirley he had a tremendous artist to help him realize the vision. Most presses at that time were not putting that kind of attention into the presentation, certainly not seeing the book cover, the design, all of it, as being a significant part of the poetry experience in the form of a book."

When Boyd began work as the editor of *Roses and Revolution: The Selected Writings of Dudley Randall*, published by Wayne State University Press in 2009, she too turned to Woodson. Her request: a book cover compelling and artful enough to capture Randall's literary legacy and his love of aesthetic beauty. Woodson responded by creating an illustration of painting and collage fused with a passage from Randall's famous *Booker T. and W.E.B.* poem in his handwriting. Shortly after its publication, the book was nominated for an NAACP Image Award.

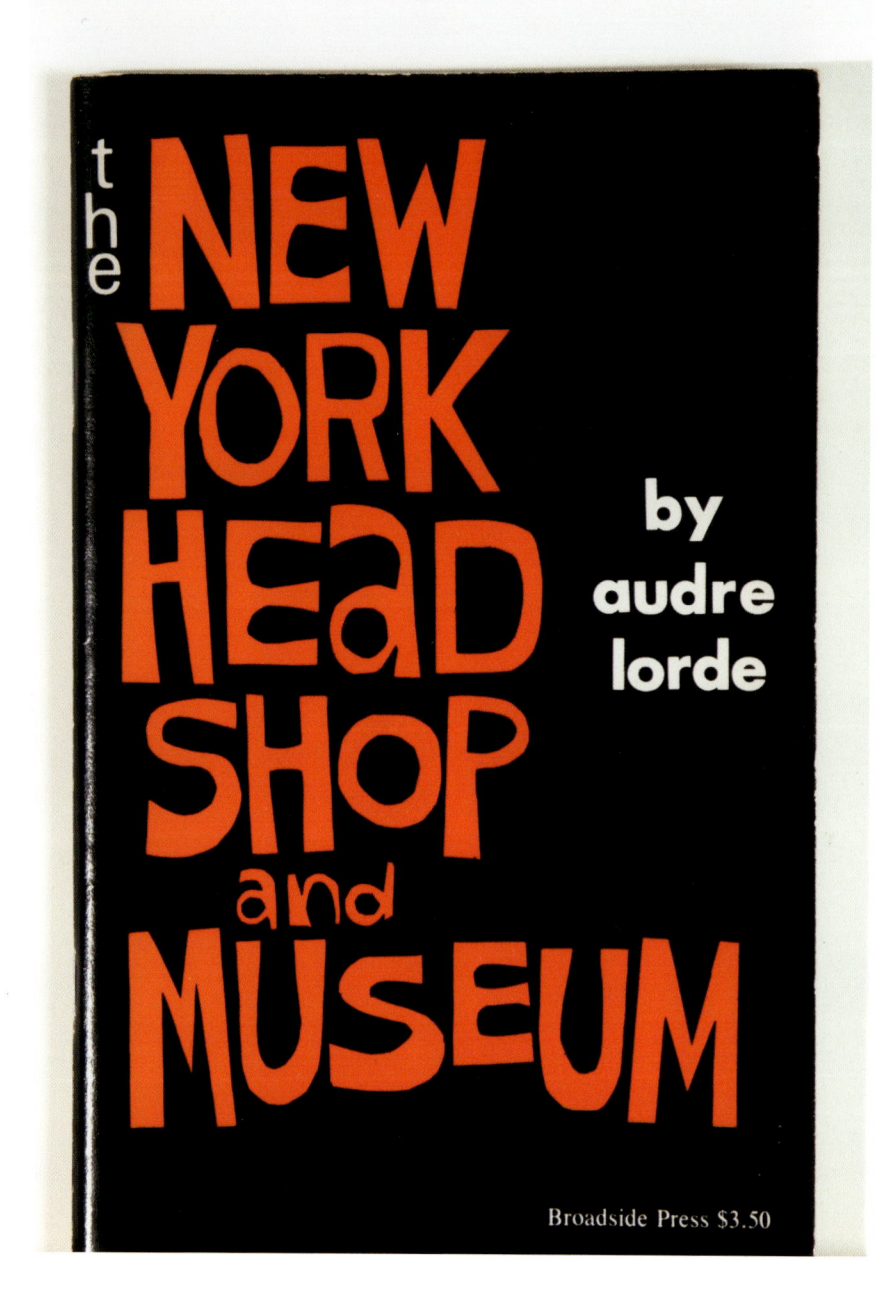

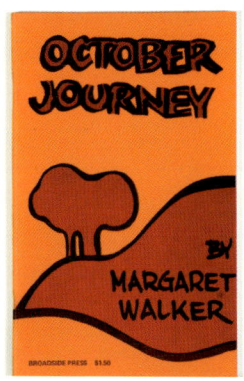

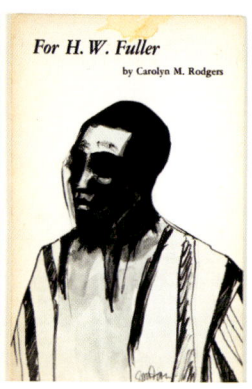

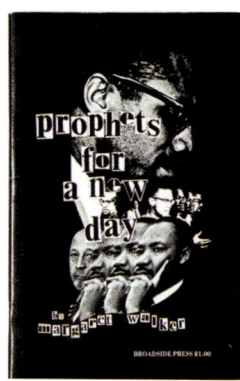

Chapbook covers designed by Shirley in the 1970s.

OPPOSITE

Rip, Rapid, Revolution (detail)
1975
Mixed media/collage
16 × 18½ in.

"When you picked up the book, if you knew anything about Dudley Randall, you knew you were holding a gift. Shirley wanted his actual handwriting, not just typed words, and that vision made the book something really special to hold, with a historical imprint from Dudley himself."

Boyd says Randall and Woodson were creative kindreds, a duo with a mutual and an inexplicable ability to express Black culture and to move it forward, artfully.

"Somehow, they each understood the interdisciplinary cross-fertilization that just naturally influences Black artists; that it's not only of value, but it makes the culture richer. And the art that comes from those many influences is something of worth, something with longevity," Boyd explains. "It's very much a part of the culture to not restrict yourself. In Shirley's paintings you have all of these connections happening in this dynamic way because she's not just connected to visual artists. She's also connected to writers, and to musicians. Everybody knows Shirley and, as a result, she knows the culture and can communicate it in everything that she does. She even had the *nerve* to give birth to an artist, Senghor."

When the grief over her father's death finally ebbed, Woodson made a key discovery. Her work with Broadside Press had provided both a refuge and the first stop on a new creative journey. The passion to paint not only resumed; a new, more intimate and experimental style using stencils instead of brushes emerged. A series of fifteen paintings entitled *Journeys* poured out. Her imagination was back and fully in flight.

If there's credit to be had, it belongs in equal parts, Woodson says, to "Dudley and Daddy," the figures who taught her to prize perseverance and purpose. "My father never let anything stop him. He wasn't an artist, but he was creative. He understood how to fit the pieces together. One time, he had three jobs and no car. He had to make his way on the bus. As an artist, you look around and you learn to use what you have, even pain," Woodson says.

"You keep going."

—**NICHOLE CHRISTIAN**

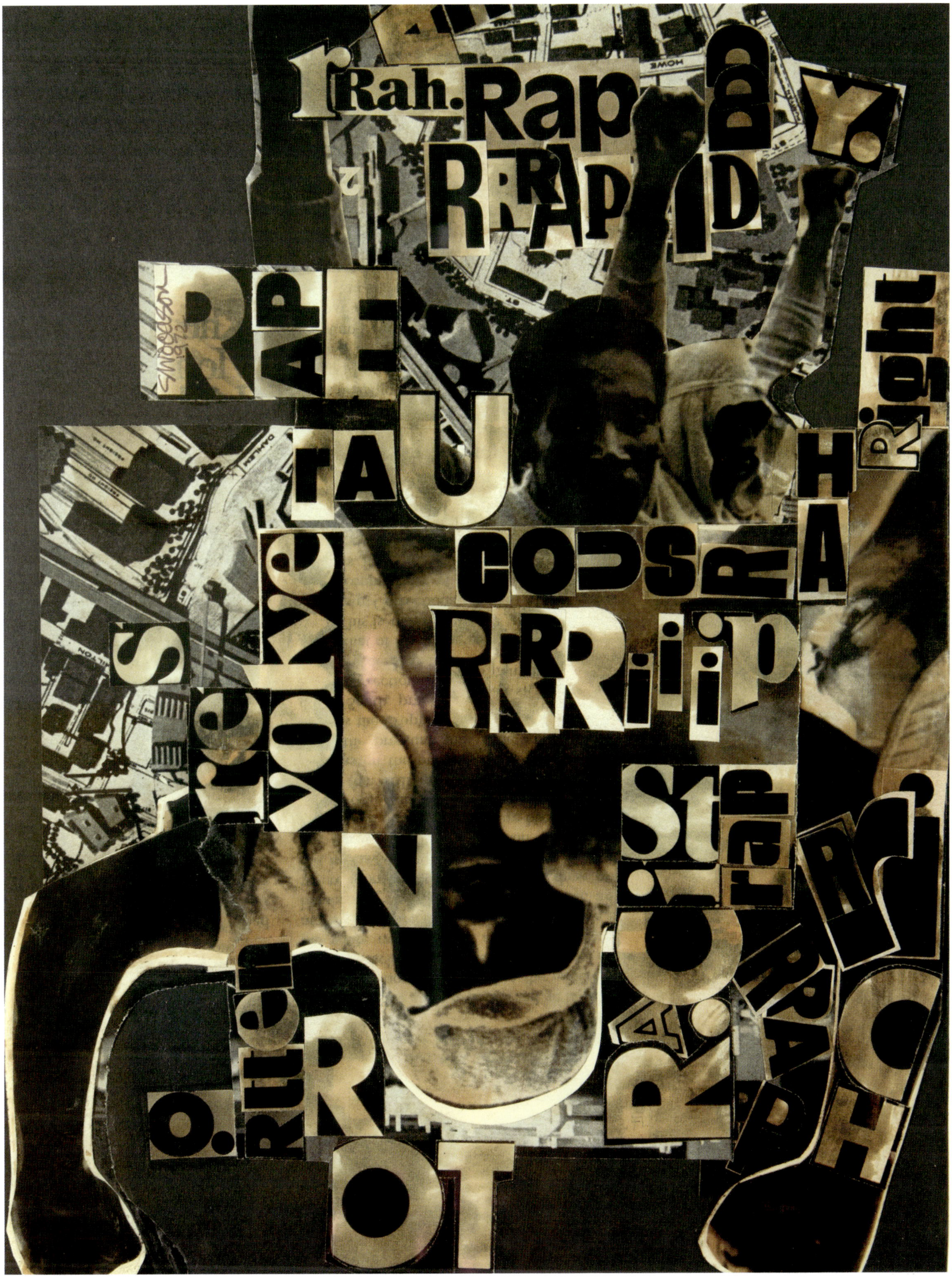
Rah.
Rap
Right
COUS

Shirley Collects

Carrie Mae Weems
After Manet
2003
Chromogenic print
33 3/16 in. dia.

Do not ask Shirley Woodson how many pieces of art she owns in her personal collection. It is not that she despises the question. She doesn't. Woodson simply does not know. Years have passed since the last attempt at a full inventory, and there are still occasional must-have artist works that must come home with her.

When the conversation about her collection and its size begins, Woodson's son Senghor Reid—the painter who is known for a keen observant eye—is at his mother's side in their shared studio. She turns to him for input, as she often does. The two trade a quick glance, but Reid is stumped too. His guess: "Endless?" The assessment is close enough. "OK," Woodson replies, "let's just say it's a lot." Mother and son seal the moment with a knowing, simultaneous burst of laughter.

For a woman known to treat every aspect of her creative life seriously, this is a rare instance of self-directed levity. In fact, Shirley Woodson—the intensely focused painter, art educator and art historian—is as purposeful, if not more so, about the artworks and style she chooses to surround herself. Each purchase is made with a surgeon's precision to some key detail.

While many collect artworks as an investment, Woodson collects to breathe, to keep her art maker's eye stimulated by colors and shapes, form and evolving culture, whatever it takes to keep art where it has always been—at the center of her world. Famously selfless and humble, Woodson concedes that the art of collecting may be the lone area of her life where she allows a bit of self-indulgence. "I love having art around me." In the house along Oakman Boulevard where Woodson and her husband, Edsel Reid, raised two sons, art is everywhere. "At one point the cars had to be parked on the street," she says with a sly smile. "You'd open the garage, and there was all of this art stored in there too."

She is unapologetic. "Just as you fill your refrigerator with food," Woodson has said, "art is necessary to feed you spiritually and culturally." In her home, few walls are bare, and stacks of art books form competing towers from the floor. "I got started in college," she recalls. At a graduate student show during her senior year, Woodson purchased a single etching. "I bought the work because I loved it and I realized that I loved having beautiful things around me." That her first purchase cost only $15 helped to fuel the decision.

Woodson still owns the etching. It lives beside an array of paintings, photographs, assemblages, drawings, ceramics, sculptures and fiber-based works bearing some of art's most vaunted names across styles and eras, primarily the creations of Black artists. You'll find the work of Elizabeth Catlett, Betye Saar, Gilda Snowden, Sam Gilliam, David Driskell, Alvin Loving. In 2019, Woodson loaned the Detroit Institute of Arts use of *After Manet,* a digital chromogenic created by Carrie Mae Weems, who is widely hailed as one of the nation's foremost contemporary artists. The work was one of 60 from 19 private collections featured in *Detroit Collects: Selections of African American Art from Private Collections*. One of her most important purchases was a steel wire necklace that incorporates okra seeds. The work was done by the late conceptual and performance artist James Lee Byars, a white classmate from her studies at Wayne State University in Detroit. "His ideas were ever expanding, and his work was just fantastic," she said. "My eye is very open. It's not just paintings that I see."

Formally, Woodson's collection is listed as the Shirley Woodson and Edsel Reid Collection, a fitting homage to the other source of her love for art collecting. "It's the way I met my husband," she explains. "He saw my work, and he bought my work. We were definitely very simpatico about spending money buying art." However, the couple had sharply

Shirley at home with some of her collection.

divergent *why*s for their shared love of, and dedication to, collecting art. "In his thinking, he believed that it was good to buy great work because then you could sell it. He was always looking ahead."

Woodson's view was always more personal. "Sell it? I'd say, 'I'm not selling any of this work.' Some artists really enjoy the work of other artists a lot. I'm getting everything from having it around me. You've got references every day, and every day there's a new relationship or detail right there. I think he understood."

Throughout her career, Woodson's approach to promoting, supporting and collecting Black art has been unceasing, albeit in her own quiet way. Generations of Black art enthusiasts and artists credit her for passing her passion on. Among them: Walter O. Evans, the man believed to own America's largest and most wide-ranging collection of Black art, has credited Woodson as a defining force. Evans had just completed medical school in Detroit. From travels to various art museums, he was developing a burgeoning interest in collecting. Then, he met Woodson through a long-forgotten mutual art friend at the DIA. In an instant, she expanded his vision.

"He says I introduced him to collecting," Woodson explains. For her part, she insists she was only encouraging him to take advantage of "a great deal" by purchasing a DIA print series named for the white abolitionist, John Brown. The story goes that Evans was not immediately sold until Woodson, with her encyclopedic knowledge of Black art and art history, explained that the series had been created by a Black man, the legendary artist Jacob Lawrence. "I told him, 'You should get this. It's important work by an important Black artist.'"

Evans agreed and called his first fine art purchase transformative. "I decided that every piece of art I would buy henceforth, would have a Black person in it," he said in celebration of the 1991 unveiling of the *Walter O. Evans Collection of African American Art* at the Beach Institute/King-Tisdell Cottage Museum in Savannah, Georgia. "What moved me was that in all my visits to the museums of the world, I almost never saw any art by African Americans. If there were any, they didn't have any Black figures in the paintings."

Partly because of her vast knowledge of Black art, Woodson was selected as the show's curator. "In his collecting of African American art, he has done so from a perspective of responsibility," she wrote in the opening curator's note. "He has responded to the visual arts as a griot, a keeper of the culture, and here he has remained steadfast."

In Shirley Woodson's words is the essence of her life's impact too.

—**NICHOLE CHRISTIAN**

Select Works, Projects and Awards

Education
MA: 1965 Wayne State University, Detroit, MI

1960 Graduate Study, Painting and Art History, School of the Art Institute of Chicago

BFA: 1958 Wayne State University

Grants and Residencies
MacDowell Colony Fellowship. Peterborough, NH, 1966

Individual Artists' Grant. Michigan Council for the Arts, 1983, 1987

Site Installation. Chene Park, Detroit, MI, 1986

Your Heritage House Museum. Detroit, MI, 1986

Creative Artists Grant. Detroit Council for the Arts, 1987

Martin Luther King, Jr., César Chávez, Rosa Parks Visiting Professor. Eastern Michigan University, Ypsilanti, MI, 1987, 1988

New Initiative for Arts Exhibition Grant. Michigan Council for the Arts, 1988, 1994, 1995, 1996

Focus Gallery. Detroit, MI, 1991

Fabric Workshop. Philadelphia, PA, 1993

Brandywine Workshop. Philadelphia, PA, 1994, 2007, 2009

Exhibitions
Solo. Arts Extended Gallery, Detroit, MI, 1963

Solo. Wayne State University Art Education Alumni, Detroit, MI, 1966

Collaboration: The Painter and The Poet, Arts Extended Gallery, Detroit, MI, 1969

Solo. *Kings and Queens*, Gallery Seven, Detroit, MI, 1970

Solo. J. Walter Thompson Advertising Agency, Detroit, MI, 1971

Solo. *Journey*, McGregor Library, Highland Park, MI, 1973

Solo. Howard University Gallery of Art, Washington, DC, 1975

Solo. *New Works/Shirley Woodson*, Automobile Club of Michigan, Dearborn, MI, 1982

Solo. *Paintings and Collages*, Your Heritage House Museum, Detroit, MI, 1984

Solo. Mercyhurst College, Erie, PA, 1985

Solo. Site Installation, Chene Park, Detroit, MI, 1986

Solo. *Paintings*, Impressions 5 Museum, Lansing, MI, 1988

Solo. *Paintings*, Eastern Michigan University, Ypsilanti, MI, 1988

Solo. *Shirley Woodson/Paintings*, University of Michigan at Flint, Flint, MI, 1989

Group. *Coast to Coast: National Women of Color*, Artist Books Traveling Nationally, 1990

Solo. *Figurations/New Paintings and Drawings*, Sherry Washington Gallery, Detroit, MI, 1992

Solo. *Paintings, Collages, Works on Paper*, Hughley Gallery and Objects, Atlanta, GA, 1992

Solo. *Current Works*, Jacobson's Home Store, Dearborn, MI, 1992

Group. United American Health Care Corporation Collection, Detroit, MI, 1993

Group. *Voices, An Artists' Book*, Nexus, Atlanta, GA, 1994

Solo. *Shirley Woodson/Collages 1982–1992*, CAAS Gallery, curated by Bamidele Demerson, University of Michigan, Ann Arbor, MI, 1994

Solo. *Shirley Woodson, Paintings, Collages/Works on Paper*, Hughley Gallery and Objects, Atlanta, GA, 1994

Group. *High Tech, Lo Tech*, Metro Center for Creative Art, curated by Robert Martin, Detroit, MI, 1995

Group. Wayne State University Arts Achievement Award Exhibition Detroit, MI, 1995

Solo. *Filament, Wanting, Memory: New Works by Shirley Woodson*, Detroit Artists Market, Detroit, MI, 1995

Duo. *Thoughts, Dreams, Visions: Paintings and Drawings* with Marva Jolly, Sculptor, Satori Fine Art, Chicago, IL, 1995

Solo. *Shirley Woodson/Figurations/New Paintings & Drawings*, Sherry Washington Gallery, Detroit, MI, 1995

Solo. *Paintings, Boxworks*, Detroit Artists Market, Detroit, MI, 1996

Solo. *Paintings*, Parish Gallery, Georgetown, Washington, DC, 1996

Two Person. *Reunion* (with Larry Walker), Camille Love Gallery, Atlanta, GA, 1996

Solo. *Recent Works*. Paintings/Drawings, Sherry Washington Gallery, Detroit, MI, 1996

Solo. Satori Fine Art, Chicago, IL, 1998

Group. *Idioms*, JRainey Gallery, Detroit, MI, 1998

Group. NCA National Exhibition, Skylight Gallery, curated by Cheryl Hanna, Brooklyn, NY, 2001,

Group. 4 Person Show, UMOJA Gallery, Southfield, MI, 2001

Duo. *Legacy* (with Senghor Reid), Ford Gallery, Wayne County Community College, Detroit, MI, 2003

Group. *Retro*, Hart Plaza Gallery, Detroit, MI, 2003

Group. *Self Portraits*, Sherry Washington Gallery, Detroit, MI, 2004

Solo. *Paintings and Collages*, Fort Valley State University, Fort Valley, GA, 2004

Solo. *Unpublished Poems, New Paintings*, Sherry Washington Gallery, Detroit, MI, 2006

Solo. *Paintings*, Susan Woodson Gallery, Chicago, IL, 2006

Solo. *Recent Works*, Parish Gallery, Washington, DC, 2007

Group. *Voices and Portfolio One*, Fayetteville Art Museum, Fayetteville, NC, 2008

Group. *Great American Cities*, Brandywine Printmaking Workshop, curated by Camille Ann Brewer, Philadelphia, PA, 2008

Group. *Women's Exhibition*, Scarab Club, Detroit, MI, 2010

Group. *A Survey of African American Images 1980–2000*, Charles H. Wright Museum of African American History, Detroit, MI, 2010

Group. *Five Artists*, Dell Pryor Galleries, Detroit, MI, 2011

Solo. *On Angel Wing: Collages*, NCA Gallery, Detroit, MI, 2012

Group. *Building of Tradition*, Dianne Whitfield Locke and Carnell Locke Collection of African American Art, Hampton Museum, Hampton University, Hampton, VA, 2013

Solo. *Recognition and Parallels*, Rosenthal Gallery, Fayetteville State University/Parish Gallery, Fayetteville, NC/Washington, DC, 2014

Group. *Text*, Brandywine Printmaking Workshop, Philadelphia, PA, 2014

Solo. *Red Lining*, Ford Gallery, curated by Jocelyn Rainey, Wayne County Community College, Detroit, MI, 2015

Duo. *Layers/Collages* (with Anita Bates), Live Coal Gallery, Detroit, MI, 2015

Group. *Peace*, Ellen Kayrod Gallery, curated by Saffell Gardner, Detroit, MI, 2016

Group. *NCA at Woodmere*, Woodmere Town Hall, curated by Cynthia Samples, Beachwood, OH, 2016

Group. *Gold Medal Exhibition*, Scarab Club, Detroit, MI, 2016

Senghor Ried's hand-colored photograph of Shirley in her home studio, made while he was an 11th grade art student at Renaissance High School.

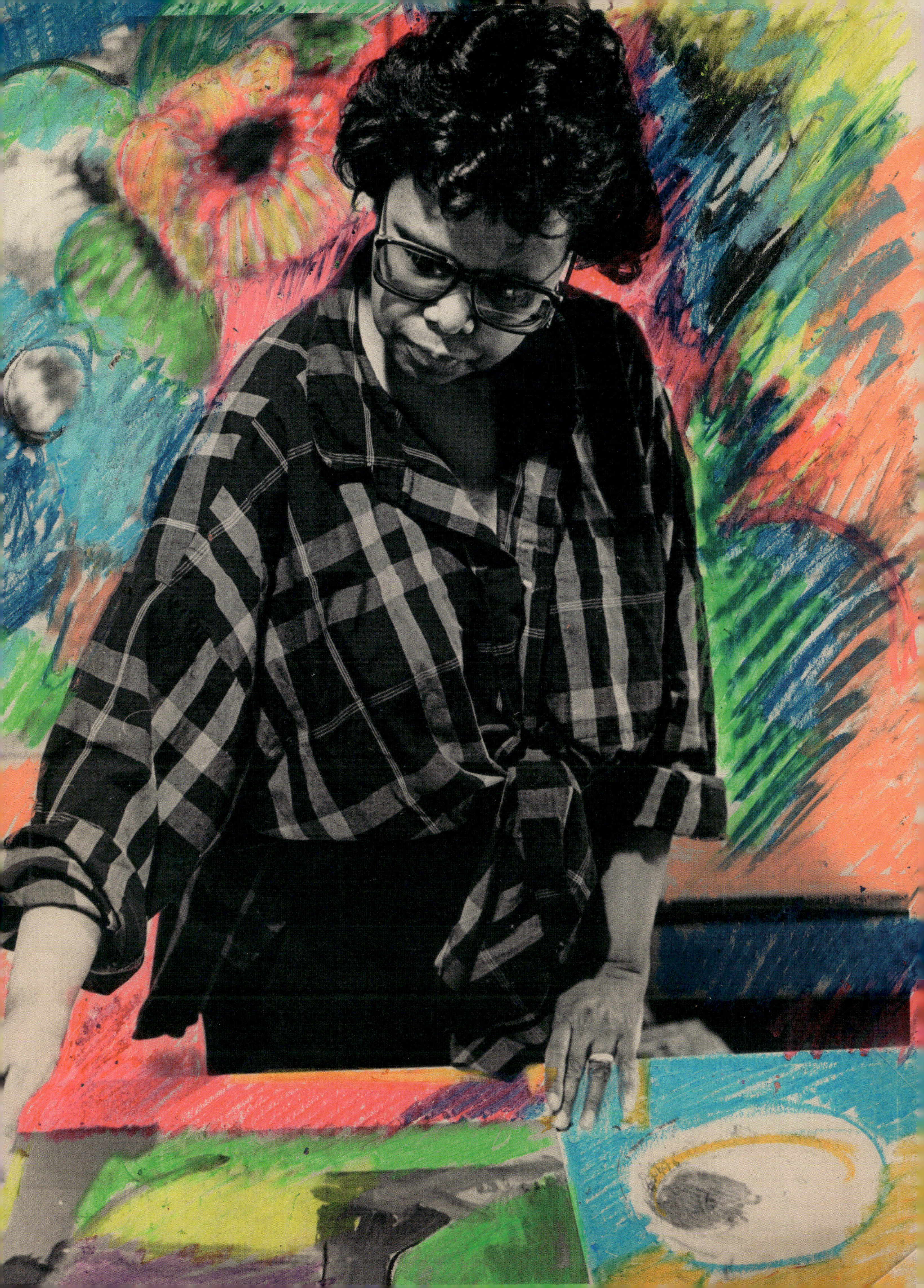

Group. *Drawing Exhibition*, Arts Extended Gallery, Detroit, MI, 2017

Group. *Six Mile Connection*, Marygrove College Gallery, Detroit, MI, Rose DeSloover, 2017

Group. *50 Years: Detroit Rebellion*, Charles H. Wright Museum of African American History, Detroit, MI, 2017

Group. *Rebellion*, Detroit Artists Market, Detroit, MI, 2017

Group. *By and About Women: Women Artists In Collection of Dr. Dianne Whitfield Locke and Dr. Carnell Locke*, Harvey Gantt Center for African American Art and Culture, curated by Michael Harris, Charlotte, NC, 2018

Group. *Spark*, Annex Gallery, Detroit, MI, 2019

Solo. *In Context: Paintings, Drawings, Collages*, Norwest Gallery, Detroit, MI, 2019

Group. *Artists and Students*, Annex Gallery, Detroit, MI, 2019

Group. *A Common Thread*, Detroit Artists Market, curated by Dell Pryor, Detroit, MI, 2020

Group. *Vision of the 44th President*, National Invitational Exhibition, Charles H. Wright Museum of African American History, Detroit, MI, 2020

Group. *Brilliance/Heritage*, NCA Gallery, Detroit, MI, 2021

Solo. Detroit Artists Market, Detroit, MI, 2021

Solo. Scarab Club, Detroit, MI, 2021

Group. *Griot Speaks*, Norwest Gallery, Detroit, MI, 2021

Group. *Art in Full Bloom*, UMOJA Gallery, Southfield, MI, 2021

Collections

Absolut, New York, NY

Amoco, Chicago, IL

Blue Cross/Blue Shield, Detroit, MI

Brandywine Workshop, Philadelphia, PA

Charles H. Wright Museum of African American History, Detroit, MI

Detroit Board of Education, Detroit, MI

Detroit Edison, Detroit, MI

Detroit Institute of Arts, Detroit, MI

Detroit Public Schools/Detroit Children's Museum, Detroit, MI

Detroit Receiving Hospital, Detroit, MI

Detroit Tigers, Detroit, MI

Dulin Gallery of Art, Knoxville, TN

Fabric Workshop and Museum, Philadelphia, PA

Florida A & M University, Tallahassee, FL

Henry Ford Hospital, Detroit, MI

Mott-Warsh Collection of Contemporary Art, Flint, MI

Museum of the National Center for Afro-American Artists, Boston, MA

Northwestern University, African American Studies Library, Evanston, IL

Ruth Chandler Williamson Gallery at Scripps College, Claremont, CA

Schomburg Center for Research in Black Culture, New York, NY

Seagram Company, Ltd., Montreal, Canada

Studio Museum in Harlem, New York

Toledo Art Commission, Toledo, Ohio

The White House, Washington, DC

United American Health Care, Detroit, MI

Wayne State University, Detroit, MI

Wellness, Inc., Detroit, MI

Your Heritage House Museum, Detroit, MI

Awards

Absolut Award, 2001

Alain Locke Award, Friends of African and African American Art, Detroit Institute of Arts, 1998

Artists Award, Friends of African and African American Art, Detroit Institute of Arts, 2008

Arts Achievement Award, Wayne State University, 1995

Children's Museum of Detroit Award for Outstanding Contribution to the Arts, 2000

Coalition of 100 Black Women, Arts and Literature Award, 1997

Distinguished Award for Pioneering in the Arts, United Black Artists, 1991

Dr. Charles H. Wright Award for Excellence for Arts in Education, 1999

Excellence in Visual Arts Award, National Conference of Artists, Michigan Chapter, 2004, 2009

First Prize Visual Arts, Toledo Arts Commission, 1984

History Makers Award, 2005

Lillian Pierce Benbow Art Award, Delta Sigma Theta Sorority, Inc., 2000

Michigan Women's Foundation, Outstanding Contribution to the Visual Arts, 1988

National Conference of Artists Award for Artistic Excellence, 1977

OBA Achievement Award, Organization of Black Alumni, Wayne State University, 2005

Purchase Award, Toledo Arts Commission, 1984

Seagrams Award, Perspectives in African-American Art, 1995

Women's Informal Network of Detroit, 1998

Graphic Design

Emanuel, James. *Panther Man*. Broadside Press, Detroit, MI, 1970 (book)

Hudson-Weems, Clenora. *Emmett Till: The Sacrificial Lamb of the Civil Rights Movement*. Bedford Press, Troy, MI, 1994 (book)

Jordan, June. "Poem: On Moral Leadership As A Political Dilemma." Broadside #78, 1971 (August)

Lorde, Audre. *The New York Head Shop and Museum*. Broadside Press, Detroit, MI, 1974 (book)

Ntiri, Daphne (editor). *Roots and Blossoms: African American Plays for Today* (Contributions to African American and African literature and studies). Bedford Press, Troy, MI, 1991 (book)

Odarty, Bill. *A Safari of African Cooking*. Broadside Press, Detroit, MI, 1976 (book)

Plumpp, Sterling. "Muslim Men." Broadside #43, 1971

Randall, Dudley. "All Dressed In Pink." Broadside #2, 1966

Randall, Dudley. "Ballad of Birmingham." Broadside #1, 1965 (September)

Randall, Dudley. *Broadside Memories: Poets I Have Known*. Broadside Press Detroit, MI, 1975, (book)

Randall, Dudley. *More To Remember*. Third World Press, Chicago, IL, 1971 (book)

Randall, Dudley. "The Six." Poster #6, 1976

Rodgers, Carolyn. "For H.W. Fuller." Broadside #50, 1971

Sanchez, Sonia. "Liberation Poem." Broadside #34, 1970

Walker, Margaret. *October Journey*. Broadside Press, Detroit, MI, 1973 (pamphlet)

Walker, Margaret. *Prophets For A New Day.* Broadside Press, Detroit, MI, 1970 (book)

Bibliography

African American Art and History Timeline, Detroit Institute of Arts, 1983

Alexander Bontemps, Arna (editor). *Forever Free: Art by African-American Women, 1862-1980, An Exhibition.* Stephenson Incorporated, Alexandria, VA, 1980,

Black Women in Michigan, 1785–1985: A Resource-Study Guide, Detroit Historical Museum, Detroit, MI, 1985

Cederholm, Theresa Dickason. *Afro-American Artists; A Bio-Bibliographical Directory.* Boston Public Library, Boston, MA, 1973

Falk, Peter H. *Who Was Who In American Art, 1564–1975: 400 Years of Artists in America*. Sound View Press, 1999

Fox, Elton C. *Black Artists of the New Generation*. Dodd Mead, 1977

Henkes, Robert. *The Art of Black American Women: Works of Twenty-four Artists of the Twentieth Century.* McFarland, 1993, Jefferson, NC

Igoe, Lynn Moody with Igoe, James. *250 Years of Afro-American Art : An Annotated Bibliography,* R.R. Bowker Co., 1981, New York, NY

Kostelanetz, Richard, Metz, Mike, and Korn, Henry (editors). *Third Assembling : A Collection of Otherwise Unpublishable Manuscripts.* Assembling Press, Brooklyn, NY, 1972

Navaretta, Cynthia. *Gumbo Ya Ya: Anthology of Contemporary African-American Women Artists*. Mid March Arts Press, 1995, New York, NY

Pack Bailey, Leaonead (editor). *Broadside Authors and Artists: An Illustrated Biographical Directory.* Broadside Press, Detroit, MI, 1974

Patterson, Lindsay (editor). *The Negro in Music and Art*. Publishers Co., New York, NY, 1969

Serendipity, Literary Art Journal, Detroit, MI, 1958

The Study of Negro Life and History International Library Series

Walter O. Evans Collection of African American Art, Les Payne; Leslie King-Hammond; Shirley Woodson; King-Tisdell Cottage Museum, Savannah, GA, 1991

The World of Who's Who of Women, International Biographical Center, Cambridge, MA, 1974–1975

Who's Who Among Black Americans. Northbrook, IL, 1976; *Who's Who Among Black Americans*, 1976–1988; Detroit, Gale Research Inc., 1990/91–1994/95

Periodicals

Charleston, Lula. "Profile Of An Artist: Shirley Woodson." *City Magazine*, November, 1986

Demerson, Bamidele. "Vivifying Power." *International Review of African American Art,* Vol. 9, No. 2, 1990

Murphy, Anthony. "Portfolio." *American Visions,* August–September, 1992

Parks, Carole A. "The Broadside Story." *Black World,* January, 1976

Patterson, Lindsay. "African-American Audiences and the Arts." *Upscale Magazine,* 1991

Patterson, Lindsay. "Corporate Buying of African American Art." *Upscale Magazine,* November, 1993

Williams, Kelly. "Michigan Watercolor Annual." *Art and Artists,* April, 1964

Critical Writing

"The AEG Experience: A Cooperative Commitment to Art." *The Journal of The National Art Education Association's Women's Caucus,* Issue No. 4, 1975

"The Art of Sonya Clark." catalog statement, exhibition catalog, Marygrove College, Detroit, MI

"The Box Works of Evangeline Montgomery." essay in exhibition catalog, Morgan State University Gallery, Baltimore, MD

"Carolyn Warfield Installation." National Conference of Arts Michigan Chapter Newsletter, Vol. 1, No. 2 1990

"Coast to Coast." *RE: Newsletter,* 1990

"History of Black Art in Michigan." *City Magazine,* March, 1987

"Middle Passage: Matrix and Memory The Art of Richard Hunt." 1991

"NCA Collective in Detroit." *International Review of African American Art*, Vol. 28, No. 4

"Notes on the Collector." Walter O. Evans Collection of African American Art, King-Tisdell Cottage Museum, Savannah, GA

Our Congratulations

The Kresge Eminent Artist Award celebrates one artist each year whose lifelong, influential work and generous contributions to the growth and vibrancy of Detroit's cultural environment are unmistakable. Without a doubt, that describes Shirley Woodson, who is revered by generations of Detroiters for her success as an artist and her exceptional commitment to ensure educational and career opportunities for all artists.

Woodson's legacy is central to Detroit's arts and culture community, which is renowned for its creativity, formal and informal support networks, and an unwavering commitment to truth, equity and justice. Painter, College for Creative Studies professor and inaugural Kresge Artist Fellow Gilda Snowden (1954–2014) is one of many notable artists who benefitted from her mentorship and advocacy. She is a Detroit legacy in her own right—the Gilda Awards are named in her honor. This relationship exemplifies the extensive impact of Woodson's lifetime of achievement.

Upon receiving the Eminent Artist award, Woodson noted that Detroit is fortunate to "have an arts community that's never stopped." In part, that is due to the decades of tireless work for which she is renowned. Her contributions are one important reason that the story of Detroit art is as inclusive and honest as it is, even with so much work left to be done.

We are grateful to the panel of Detroit artists and arts professionals for their dedication and wisdom in their selection. We are honored to celebrate Shirley Woodson as the 13th Kresge Eminent Artist.

—**CHRISTINA DEROOS**
DIRECTOR
KRESGE ARTS IN DETROIT

Recognizing Shirley Woodsons's career as a renowned painter, fierce advocate of arts education and mentorship, and a cultivator of creative opportunities for all, makes her selection to receive the 2021 Kresge Eminent Artist Award indisputable.

Mentorship and mutual support among artists are among the reasons why Detroit has maintained such a vibrant arts community through the decades. Within Shirley's legacy of mentorship is her relationship to Gilda Snowden. Gilda was an exceptionally accomplished, beloved, and influential artist, a professor at CCS and inaugural Kresge Artist Fellow. She was so renowned for her support of other artists that Kresge Arts in Detroit's Gilda Awards are named in her honor. Mentorship and mutual support are among the reasons Detroit has maintained a vibrant arts and culture community.

For decades, Woodson's instruction of art students and upcoming art professionals has anchored and shaped arts and culture in Detroit. For the art and design students who attend CCS—and for all of us—Woodson is an inspiring example of an artist-educator's relentless dedication and lasting impact on the trajectory of an entire community. It is an honor to administer Kresge Arts in Detroit on behalf of The Kresge Foundation, and to celebrate Shirley Woodson as the 2021 Kresge Eminent Artist.

— **DON TUSKI**
PRESIDENT
COLLEGE FOR CREATIVE STUDIES

The Kresge Eminent Artist Award and Winners

The 2021 Kresge Eminent Artist Selection Committee

Shirley Woodson was named the 2021 recipient of the Kresge Eminent Artist Award by a distinguished group of artists and arts professionals.

CHRIS HANDYSIDE Writer; musician; author; board member, Detroit Sound Conservancy

GLORIA HOUSE, PhD Poet; educator; essayist; political activist; professor emerita, University of Michigan-Dearborn; associate professor emerita, Wayne State University; Kresge Eminent Artist, 2019

CAROLE MORISSEAU Visual artist; dancer; Fulbright Hays Fellow; art professor, Wayne State University; founder and director, Detroit City Dance Co.

KENNETH MORRIS Director of evaluation and research, Detroit Institute of Arts

DELL PRYOR Founder and director, Dell Pryor Gallery

The Kresge Eminent Artist Award

Established in 2008, the Kresge Eminent Artist Award honors an exceptional literary, fine, film or performing artist whose influential body of work, lifelong professional achievements and proven, continued commitment to the Detroit cultural community are evident. The Kresge Eminent Artist Award celebrates artistic innovation and rewards integrity and depth of vision with the financial support of $50,000. The Kresge Eminent Artist Award is unrestricted and is given annually to an artist who has lived and worked in Wayne, Oakland or Macomb counties for a significant number of years. The Kresge Eminent Artist Award, annual Kresge Artist Fellowships, Gilda Awards, and multiyear grants to arts and cultural organizations in metropolitan Detroit constitute Kresge Arts in Detroit, the foundation's core effort to provide broad support to the regional arts community. The College for Creative Studies administers the Kresge Eminent Artist Award on behalf of The Kresge Foundation.

Complimentary copies of this monograph and others in the Kresge Eminent Artist series are available while supplies last.
All monographs are also available for download.
Visit kresge.org or scan the QR code at right for more information.

About The Kresge Foundation

The Kresge Foundation was founded in 1924 to promote human progress. Today, Kresge fulfills that mission by building and strengthening pathways to opportunity for low-income people in America's cities, seeking to dismantle structural and systemic barriers to equality and justice. Using a full array of grant, loan and other investment tools, Kresge invests more than $160 million annually to foster economic and social change.

Board of Trustees

Elaine D. Rosen, Board Chair
Michael Barr
James L. Bildner
Richard Buery Jr.
Kathy Ko Chin
John Fry
Paul Hillegonds
Cynthia L. Kresge
Cecilia Muñoz
Maria Otero
Paula B. Pretlow
Nancy Schlichting
Suzanne Shank
Rip Rapson, President and CEO (Ex-Officio)

Publication Team

JENNIFER KULCZYCKI Director, External Affairs & Communications
JULIE A. BAGLEY Assistant, External Affairs & Communications
W. KIM HERON Senior Communications Officer, External Affairs & Communications
ALEJANDRO HERRERA Graphic Designer, External Affairs & Communications

Creative Team

NICHOLE CHRISTIAN Creative Director & Editor
PATRICK BARBER Art Director & Designer

Previous Kresge Eminent Artist Award Recipients

Marie Woo, 2020

Gloria House, 2019

Wendell Harrison, 2018

Patricia Terry-Ross, 2017

Leni Sinclair, 2016

Ruth Adler Schnee, 2015

Bill Rauhauser, 2014

David DiChiera, 2013

Naomi Long Madgett, 2012

Bill Harris, 2011

Marcus Belgrave, 2009

Charles McGee, 2008

Index

This index is sorted letter-by-letter. Italic page locators indicate images on the page.

A

African American art. *See* Black artists and art history; Black Arts Movement
African history, 33, 36–37, 52–53
After Manet (Weems; 2003), 68, *68*
Agee, Alice, *19*
"ancestors," art content and themes, 48, 53, 60, *60–63*
Ancestors Known (1981), *62*
Ancestors Known and Unknown (series), 60
Aretha the Queen (1969), *8*
art books, 23, 25–26, 36, 60
art collections
    personal, 68–69, *69*
    of Woodson's works, 24, 72
Art Institute of Chicago, 20
artistic research and symbolism, 33, 36–37, 48, 49, 53
Arts Extended Gallery, *17,* 23–24, *28*
art spaces. *See* galleries and art spaces; specific places
awards
    literary, 64, 65
    of Woodson, 6, 14–15, 28–29, 70, 72, 74–76

B

Bates, Anita, *21*
Bathers in Yellow Landscape (2008), *59*
Bather with Angel Wing, *2*
Biafra, 36–37, 52–53
Biafra Cries, The Thrill Is Gone (1970), *34–35, 36,* 36–37, *37*
Black artists and art history
    book publishing and titles, 23, 25–26, 33, 36, 60, 64–66, 73
    collections, 68–69
    educational inclusion, 6, 21–22, 25–26, 44, 48–49
    work and influences, 6, 23–24, 25–26, 31, 33, 40–41, 45, 48–49, 52–53, 66, 68–69
Black Arts Movement, 22–23, 64
Bolden, John, 12, 14, 15
book arts and design, 64–66, *66,* 73
Boyd, Melba Joyce, 65–66
Brewer, Camille Ann, *21,* 36–37
Broadside Press, 64–66, 73
Byars, James Lee, 68

C

Cassells, Halima Afi, 26, 28
Christian, Nichole, 10–29, 31, 64–66
Coast to Coast, a Women of Color National Artists Book Project, 60
collections
    personal, 68–69, *69*
    of Woodson's art, 24, 72
College for Creative Studies (CCS), 48–49, 75, 76
colors
    use and symbolism, 22, 48, 52, 53
    Woodson critiques and discussion, 31, 33, 37, 40, 48, 52, 53, 56
communities, art. *See* Detroit, Michigan; galleries and art spaces; Woodson, Shirley
Crossroads at Sea (2008), *57*

D

Day, Paralee, 21
deRoos, Christina, 74
Detroit, Michigan
    art galleries and spaces, *17,* 23–24, 26, *27,* 28, *28,* 29, 33, 40–41, 44, 68, 74
    history and events, 25, 29
    populations and growth, 22–23
    Woodson education career, 21–22, 25
    Woodson family relocation, 16–17
    Woodson youth and education, 18–21
Detroit Artists Market, 29
Detroit Institute of Arts (DIA), 18, 23, *28,* 68, 69
Detroit Public Schools
    art teachers and administrators, 6, 21, 44, 49
    Woodson education, 18, 20

E

Evans, Walter O., 69
Evening Glow (2012), *39,* 40, *40*

F

Fair, Valerie, *21*
Figure on the Porch (1964), *30*
Flight into Egypt No. 1 (1970), *51, 52,* 52–53
Flight into Egypt No. 3 (2006), *57*
Flight into Egypt No. 8 (2006), *56*
For Grandmother Rebecca (2003), *61*
Four at Sea (2008), *59*

G

galleries and art spaces
    access, equality, and community, 23–24, 26, 27, 33, 40–41, 44
    artists' views, 44
    curators' views, 40–41, 44, 69
Grandmother with Cloud Cover (2015), *63*
Graves, Leslie, *49*
grief, 64, 65, 66

H

Harold Neal and Detroit African American Artists, 1945 Through the Black Arts Movement (Myers), 23
"He Wrote Our History In Light" (poem), 64
Highland Park Public Schools, 6, 21, 65
House, Gloria, 15, 64, *77*
Hughes, Langston, 23

I

Igbo people, 36–37, 52–53

J

"journeys," art content and themes, 56–57
Journeys (series), *18,* 66
Joy, Grief and the Artist (1969), *11,* 24

K

Kresge Foundation Eminent Artist Award, 6, 74, 76
    previous recipients, 15, 64, *77*
    Woodson (2021), 6, 14–15, 28–29, 74–75
Kresge Gilda Awards, 31, 74, 75

L
Lawrence, Jacob, 69
literature: publishing and design, 64–66, *66*, 73
Live Coal Gallery, 44
Lorde, Audre, 65, *66*

M
Martha's Vandellas (1969), *32*, 33
McDaniel, Robin, 21–22
McGhee, Allie, 33
Myers, Julia R., 23

N
National Conference of Artists, 26, 28, 41, 44
Neal, Harold, 23, 33
Nelson, Sabrina, *21*
Nigerian Civil War, 36–37, 52–53

O
On the Beach (1959), *58*

P
Phifer, Priscilla A., *29*
poetry, 64, 65–66
Pryor, Dell, 18, *28,* 40–41, *41*
Pulaski, Tennessee, 16–17

R
racism and racial exclusion, art world, 23, 26, 33
Rainey, Jocelyn, 48–49, *49*
Randall, Dudley, 64–66, *65,* 73
Rapson, Rip, 6, 15
Re-entry (2014–2020), *47, 48,* 48–49
Re-entry With Shell (detail) (2014), *4*
Reid, Dayton, 28, 44, *45*
Reid, Edsel, 24–26, *25, 26, 27,* 28, 65, 68–69
Reid, Khari, *20, 24, 24, 25, 27,* 28, *45,* 64
Reid, Senghor, 12, 24, 66, 68
  art career and works, 41, 44, 53, *55, 71*
  essay, 52–53
  photographs, *20, 24, 25, 27*
Rip, Rapid, Revolution (1975), *67*
Rock, Yvette, 44–45
Roses and Revolution: The Selected Writings of Dudley Randall (2009), 65–66
The Ruling Class: Shirley Woodson (Reid; 2021), *55*

S
Scarab Club, 29
Self Portrait with Studio (1968), *15*
Self Portrait with Teeth (1964), *13*
Shield of the Nile No. 2 (1969), *7*
Snowden, Gilda, *21, 29,* 31, 44, 48–49, 60, 74, 75

T
Taylor, Cledie, 18, *19,* 23–24, *28*
Thayer, Nancy, 44
Their Names are On My Lips (2002), *60*
Trent, Kimberly, 28
Tuski, Don, 75

W
Washington, Sherry, 24
"water," art content and themes, *7,* 48, *57–59,* 58
Wayne State University, 20, 25, 72
Weems, Carrie Mae, 68, *68*
We Were on the Island (2008), *43, 44,* 44–45
white exclusiveness and exclusion, art world, 23, 26, 33
white supremacist groups, 16
Woodson, Azzie Lee, 16
Woodson, Celia Trotter, 16–18, *17,* 20, 52
Woodson, Charlotte, 16
Woodson, Claude, 16–17, *17,* 20, 64, 66
Woodson, Curtis, 17, *17,* 24, 25
Woodson, Emily, 16
Woodson, Shirley
  artistic themes, 31, 33, 36–37, 40, 45, 48, 52–53, 56, 58, 60
  artist statement, 9
  awards, 6, 14–15, 28–29, 70, 72, 74–76
  biography and family, 16–18, *17,* 24–28, 44, 52, 60, 64, 66, 68
  career, 6, 12, 14–15, 21–24, 25, 26–29, 31–53, 56–67, 68, 69, 70, 72–73, 75
  colleagues' favorite works, and tributes, 31–53
  collection, 68–69, *69*
  as community cultural influence, 12, 14–15, 23–24, 26, 28, 33, 40–41, 44, 66, 69, 74, 75
  creative/work processes, 12, 21, 25, 29, 31, 33, 36, 37, 40, 48, 49, 60, 64–65, 66, 68
  education and training, 14, 18–21, 22–24, 25, 70
  exhibitions, 23–24, 29, 40, 44, 64–65, 70, 72
  photographs, *9, 14, 16, 17, 18, 19, 20, 21, 24, 25, 26, 27, 28, 29, 30, 45, 49, 65, 69, 71*
  Salon (curated selections), *56–63*

Y
Youngblood, Elizabeth, 14–15, 21

List of Works

Ancestors Known (1981), 62
Aretha the Queen (1969), 8
Bathers in Yellow Landscape (2008), 59
Bather with Angel Wing, front and back covers, 2
Biafra Cries, The Thrill Is Gone (1970), 34–37
Crossroads at Sea (2008), 57
Evening Glow (2012), 39, 40
Figure on the Porch (1964), 30
Flight into Egypt No. 1 (1970), 51, 52
Flight into Egypt No. 3 (2006), 57
Flight into Egypt No. 8 (2006), 56
For Grandmother Rebecca (2003), 61
Four at Sea (2008), 59
Grandmother with Cloud Cover (2015), 63
Joy, Grief and the Artist (1969), 11, 24
Martha's Vandellas (1969), 32
On the Beach (1959), 58
Re-entry (2014–2020), 47, 48
Re-entry With Shell (detail) (2014), 4
Rip, Rapid, Revolution (1975), 67
Self Portrait with Studio (1968), 15
Self Portrait with Teeth (1964), 13
Shield of the Nile No. 2 (1969), 7
Their Names are On My Lips (2002), 60
We Were on the Island (2008), 43, 44
Why Do I Delight (1995), 61

Photography Credits

Unless otherwise noted, photos used throughout this monograph are from the personal collection of Shirley Woodson. Every effort has been made to locate and credit the holders of copyrighted materials.

Photography credits by photographer

Akpan, Kwadwo O. Page 65
Barber, Patrick 9
Cancelosi, Jeff 28 (top), 29 (bottom), 41, 45, 49
Gowman, Kate 69
Grannum, Hugh 27 (top)
Jones, Ralph 27 (bottom), 28 (bottom), 29 (top)
Randall, Dudley 26
Reid, Edsel 14, 18 (bottom), 21 (top), 24
Reid, Senghor 71
Sanders, Bill 21 (bottom)
Taylor, Cledie 25 (top)
Watson, Susan 25 (bottom)
Wilson, James D. 17, 30

Rights information

Page 68 The J. Paul Getty Museum, Los Angeles
Carrie Mae Weems, *After Manet*, 2003, chromogenic print, 33 3/16 in. dia.